EXPLORATORY THOUGHTS ON LUKE

A SURGEON EXAMINES A
PHYSICIAN'S GOSPEL

Exploratory Thoughts on Luke

*A Surgeon examines a
Physician's Gospel*

by Jonathan Redden

Christian Year Publications

ISBN-13: 978 1 872734 44 6

Typeset by John Ritchie Ltd., Kilmarnock
Printed by Bell & Bain Ltd., Glasgow

Contents

Preface

The Gospels have been much-loved books for scores of generations. They have given encouragement and hope to believers and brought enquiring readers and hearers to faith. The third Gospel is a masterpiece of history, theology and emotional joy.

The author weaves a story of Jesus, in which many different people encounter Christ. These were often the least esteemed in the ancient world. They were women, children, foreigners, and the sick. All of them were treated with special respect and compassion. Furthermore, the writer was clearly interested in the details of the healing miracles.

It is generally agreed that the author of the third Gospel is the same as that of the Acts of the Apostles. Until the early twentieth century, the author was understood to be Luke. However, in recent decades, some scholars have questioned this consensus, perhaps in search of something new to say.

In spite of this, there is still good evidence that Luke was the author and he is referred to as "the beloved physician". (Colossians 4:14) All the early writers and church Fathers testify to that view.

Why would this have been so if another individual had been the author? There would have been more publicity if a better known person within the early church had been awarded the title.

It is thought that Luke was a Greek physician although some have suggested that he was a Hellenistic Jew. The earliest reference to him outside the Scriptures is probably from the second century.

Luke, was born in <u>Antioch</u>, by profession, was a physician. He had become a disciple of the apostle Paul and later followed Paul until his [Paul's] martyrdom. Having served the <u>Lord</u> continuously, unmarried *and without children, filled with the <u>Holy Spirit</u> he died at the age of 84 years. (Anti-Marcionite prologue to the Gospel of Luke)*

Medicine and surgery in the first century was not just a system of magic although there were many charlatans around. (Acts 13:6) Physicians and surgeons were often skilled in their use of herbs and opium, for example. Surgical procedures were surprisingly advanced. Galen (c. 129-199 A.D.) carried out cataract surgery and advised meticulous cleanliness to prevent contagion.

At the same time there were also Jewish physicians. It is worth noting that in the first five books of the Bible there are 613 commandments, of which 213 are of a medical and preventative nature.

Down the centuries, doctors have felt an identity with Luke. Christians in particular have considered their vocation in medicine to be alongside of that of Luke. It is as if there is a Gospel association.

In some respects it is surprising that to date, as far as I am aware, no Christian doctor has written a commentary on Luke. It is impossible to add to the literary and language details of what has already been written by New Testament scholars, but these *"Exploratory Thoughts"* lie in the gap between simple notes and the more analytical commentaries. They are mainly concerned with application rather than description and explanation. The physician and surgeon are often asked to give advice on many associated matters not necessarily directly clinical. Luke is full of stories that fall into that category. These *"Thoughts"* are often more expansive on the medical issues presented than other commentaries.

In his writings, Luke says very little about himself or his life as a physician. His purpose is to emphasize Jesus Christ in whom he came to believe and whom he served.

Although there are always bound to be some disagreements, I am grateful to the writers of other commentaries. They have been included in the bibliography and, with all the preachers I have had the privilege to hear, they have been most helpful.

I am grateful to my friends, and the staff of the publishers, Ritchie

Christian Media, Alison Banks, Alan Cameron and Fraser Munro, and particularly Jane my wife for their encouragement and comments.

It is our prayer that those who read these thoughts will be helped and strengthened in their Christian journey. If there are readers who have not yet committed themselves to Christ in a personal way, I hope that they will read Luke's Gospel with wonder, as I did at the age of twelve and be enabled to say 'Yes!' to the invitation of Jesus to follow Him.

Bibliography

Barker, Kenneth, (Ed.) *The NIV Study Bible* (London: Hodder and Stoughton, 1990)

Caird, G. B. *Saint Luke* (Harmondsworth: Penguin Books, 1975)

Carson, D. A., *Scandalous* (Nottingham: Inter-Varsity Press, 2010)

Elwell, Walter A., (Ed) *Evangelical Dictionary of Theology* (Grand Rapids: Baker Acaademic, 2001)

Geldenhuys, Norval, *The Gospel of Luke* (London: Marshall, Morgan and Scott, 1977)

Gooding, David, *According to Luke* (Coleraine: The Myrtlefield Trust, 2013)

Guy H. A., *The Gospel of Luke* (London: MacMillan, 1972)

MacArthur, John, *The MacArthur Study Bible* (Nashville: Thomas Nelson, 1997)

Manson, William, *The Gospel of Luke* (London: Hodder and Stoughton, 1945)

Morris, Leon, *Luke, An Introduction and Commentary* (Leicester: Inter-Varsity Press, 1989)

Munro, Fraser, A., *The Folly of Atheism* (Kilmarnock: Ritchie Christian Media, 2013)

Ryle, J. C. *Expository Thoughts on Luke, Volume One* (Edinburgh: Banner of Truth Trust, 1986)

Ryle, J. C. *Expository Thoughts on Luke, Volume Two* (Edinburgh: Banner of Truth Trust, 1986)

Short, A. Rendle, *The Bible and Modern Medicine* (Exeter: The Paternoster Press, 1966)

Wilcock, Michael, *The Message of Luke* (Leicester: Inter-Varsity Press, 1997)

Wright, Tom, *Luke for Everyone* (London: SPCK, 2004)

Luke 1:1-4

1 Inasmuch as many have taken in hand to set in order a narrative of those things which have been fulfilled among us, 2 just as those who from the beginning were eyewitnesses and ministers of the word delivered them to us, 3 it seemed good to me also, having had perfect understanding of all things from the very first, to write to you an orderly account, most excellent Theophilus, 4 that you may know the certainty of those things in which you were instructed.

Luke wrote in a first century world that was becoming progressively hostile towards Christians. The Roman authorities initially regarded Christians as part of a Jewish sect. The Jews had special recognition and therefore a measure of protection under the Roman Empire, but that was changing. Christians, with the ever-increasing number of non-Jewish adherents, were being seen as a separate entity. They were now experiencing new dangers, and because of their different lifestyle, all sorts of grotesque and damaging rumours circulated.

It was in that context that Luke wrote his Gospel. It was directed to Theophilus, in order to clarify accounts about Jesus and to encourage belief.

The first four verses, known as the prologue, are the only verses in the New Testament that are written in a classical Greek style. This gives an indication that Luke did not wish to have only one reader but that the whole world should know. Little did he realise that one day his readership would indeed stretch around the globe.

As far as Christians in the West are concerned, we are now facing a religious crisis. In the United Kingdom, half the population consider themselves as non-religious. To many, Christianity is associated with discrimination, child abuse, brain-washing, marginalisation of women, and fantastical beliefs. It belongs to a bygone age and has lost its relevance in the contemporary world. There have always been critics, but now their voices have become more vociferous, strident, and increasingly bitter. There are some, in their antipathy to Christianity, who even assert that Jesus never existed. In their brash confidence they go contrary to all the available and reasonable evidence.

Luke set out his position as having examined carefully all the accessible documents. He received testimony from eyewitnesses. He had conversations with the leadership of this new movement.

Luke speaks to us today in our efforts to counter the rumours and myths about modern perceptions of Christianity. As in every age, Christians have an enormous task. As the West becomes increasingly suspicious and dismissive of Christians and our world-view, we need to remember that God is in control. We may feel that we are the losers and that the prevailing opinion is against us, but history tells us and God promises us that the ultimate victory is His.

We see in this and the other Gospels that Jesus appeals to every kind of person, high and low, old and young, rich and poor, female and male, military and civilian, educated and not so well educated, the imaginative and the down-to-earth, the respectable and those who are considered disreputable.

We must always remember that Christianity is not a mere life-coach instructional manual, or a series of lifestyle ideas, but is based on a person who lived, and historical facts surrounding that life. Luke and the other Gospel writers wanted to express more than facts. They also wanted to bring meaning to those facts so that lives could be changed and transformed towards that person God has intended us to be.

Men and women need to respond to more than a story. They need to ask God to reveal a new relationship that can only be found in Jesus.

Luke's friend and mentor, the Apostle Paul, put the issue succinctly to the Thessalonians a number of years before Luke put pen to parchment:

For our gospel did not come to you in word only, but also in power, and in the Holy Spirit and in much assurance...And you became followers of us and of the Lord, having received the word in much affliction, with joy of the Holy Spirit. (1 Thess. 1: 5-6)

Luke was very careful and rigorous in his treatment of the available material, (v.3) but he was not a dispassionate observer from the outside looking in. Although he had never met Jesus during His earthly ministry, he believed in Christ and was transformed into the theologian, historian, pastor, and beloved physician he became.

This Gospel or good news will become more readily understood and delighted in as we read further in the pages of this unfolding story.

Luke 1:5-13

5 There was in the days of Herod, the king of Judea, a certain priest named Zacharias, of the division of Abijah. His wife *was* of the daughters of Aaron, and her name *was* Elizabeth. 6 And they were both righteous before God, walking in all the commandments and ordinances of the Lord blameless. 7 But they had no child, because Elizabeth was barren, and they were both well advanced in years. 8 So it was, that while he was serving as priest before God in the order of his division, 9 according to the custom of the priesthood, his lot fell to burn incense when he went into the temple of the Lord. 10 And the whole multitude of the people was praying outside at the hour of incense. 11 Then an angel of the Lord appeared to him, standing on the right side of the altar of incense. 12 And when Zacharias saw *him*, he was troubled, and fear fell upon him. 13 But the angel said to him, "Do not be afraid, Zacharias, for your prayer is heard; and your wife Elizabeth will bear you a son, and you shall call his name John.

The story does not begin straightaway with an introduction to Jesus, but with an aging couple who in the normal run of things would not have disturbed the pages of history. The powerful "movers and shakers" were Herod in Jerusalem and the Emperor Caesar in Rome.

The difference between Herod and Zacharias and Elizabeth could not be more obvious. Herod was a gifted diplomat, ruler and military leader. He was also a ruthless, cruel psychopath. In the course of his life, he murdered his wife, his three sons, mother-in-law, brother-in-law, uncle and many others. He was feared, hated and not mourned at his death. Herod and Caesar were the ones who attracted the headlines. In contrast, Zacharias and Elizabeth were devout, principled, law-abiding and unknown. In God's eyes, they were the more important and their contribution far more significant.

Christians often think that they do not count for much, but it is Christian witness and service that really changes people and the world for good. Celebrities may set fashions, politicians may make policies and legislators may pass laws, but it is God's people who can make the difference that counts in eternity.

Zacharias and Elizabeth were both of a priestly line and family and it was crucial that the line continued. Priests had to come from the line of Aaron or they would cease to exist. It was therefore all the more of a heartache that she could not conceive and give birth to a son. In those days it was felt that someone must have done something wrong to cause infertility.

Every month this couple would have prayed and grieved but somehow they kept going and lived exemplary lives and served God faithfully. Although priests were not allowed to marry a divorcee (Leviticus 21:7), they themselves might divorce and remarry. If Zacharias was a man of the world, he could have easily "thrown over" Elizabeth and married a "younger model". I have seen that happen so often when men have reached the heights of their profession or business.

There are few couples in the Bible who could be regarded as role models. Many of the Old Testament heroes had flawed marriages. The three notable marriages in the New Testament are this elderly couple, Mary and Joseph, and Priscilla and Aquila who appear in Acts and the Pauline epistles.

In these pages we note some qualities in this godly couple.

Firstly, they were both believers. They had a common key interest and motivation. Their goals were the same. Whilst there are numerous marriages where Christians are married to non-Christians, the Bible urges us to marry Christian believers. (2 Corinthians 6: 14) Marrying a Christian is not necessarily the guarantee of a good marriage, but it is a step in the right direction.

Secondly, they were a couple who confided with one another. They were able to share their deepest thoughts and concerns. They appeared to enjoy one another's company.

Thirdly, they kept together during hard times. This is particularly clear during Elizabeth's childlessness and also when Zacharias was later disabled in his speech.

There were between eight and eighteen thousand priests in Israel. Their duties were concerned with instruction of the people and ceremonial duties in the Jerusalem Temple. It was a chance in a lifetime when Zacharias was chosen to burn incense on the appointed day.

It was during his service that an extraordinary incident took place.

Modern men and women have great difficulty in believing in the described angelic visitation. If we do not believe in a creator God then it is unlikely that we will believe in the truth of such an event. The main problem is not difficulty over the text but initial belief in God. We often think that supernatural claims like this were common in Israel at that time, but angelic visions had not happened for centuries.

Zacharias was terrified. That was a frequent emotion when the Bible describes a divine revelation or appearance, not laughter, not fascination, not a warm spiritual feeling but unmodified terror. We then read words which are so typical, and would be repeated regularly in the ministry of Jesus, "Do not be afraid." Or more succinctly, "Fear not!"

We are so often fearful of people around us, frightened by our circumstances, uncertain about the future, and need to remind ourselves of those comforting and encouraging words.

After all those years of prayer, the old man heard words that shocked him profoundly. He and Elizabeth were going to have a son who would be named John.

Before moving on to the next passage, it is worth stating that while angelic visions may not be part of our every day experience, there are an increasing number of unconnected reports of dreams and visions experienced by Muslims in the Middle East and other parts of the world. They appear to see Jesus who invites them to follow Him. There are now thousands who have become Christian in this way. It is not a phenomenon we broadcast or exaggerate, but it should be noted.

Luke 1:14-25

14 And you will have joy and gladness, and many will rejoice at his birth. **15** For he will be great in the sight of the Lord, and shall drink neither wine nor strong drink. He will also be filled with the Holy Spirit, even from his mother's womb. **16** And he will turn many of the children of Israel to the Lord their God. **17** He will also go before Him in the spirit and power of Elijah, 'to turn the hearts of the fathers to the children,' and the disobedient to the wisdom of the just, to make ready a people prepared for the Lord." **18** And Zacharias said to the angel, "How shall I know this? For I am an old man, and my wife is well advanced in years." **19** And the angel answered and said to him, "I am Gabriel, who stands in the presence of God, and was sent to speak to you and bring you these glad tidings. **20** But behold, you will be mute and not able to speak until the day these things take place, because you did not believe my words which will be fulfilled in their own time." **21** And the people waited for Zacharias, and marveled that he lingered so long in the temple. **22** But when he came out, he could not speak to them; and they perceived that he had seen a vision in the temple, for he beckoned to them and remained speechless. **23** So it was, as soon as the days of his service were completed, that he departed to his own house. **24** Now after those days his wife Elizabeth conceived; and she hid herself five months, saying, **25** "Thus the Lord has dealt with me, in the days when He looked on *me*, to take away my reproach among people."

These verses tell us about the characteristics and purpose of Zacharias and Elizabeth's coming son. He is to be the link between the prophets and the imminent Messiah. The previous prophet was Malachi and then silence for four hundred years. John was to be the last member of that tradition. The angel told the amazed old man what his son would achieve.

Virtually all new-born babies are a delight and cause for celebration. John would be more so. From these verses we learn about the nature and qualities of this coming prophet.

Firstly, he would be great in the sight of God. Many aspire to be famous or great in the sight of the world. They wish some day to inhabit the pages of the celebrity magazines, or achieve an online story that will "go viral". Greatness in God's eyes may mean becoming well-known, but it is principally a life of faith and trust. It can be an unpopular way. It may be unsung by thousands. It is not only a life of challenge and occasional trial, but it is also a life of joy and peace. We may do things that we never thought were possible. We should do our best to be great in the eyes of God.

Secondly, the prophet was called to be separate from the world. We learn later that he lived a rugged life in the desert with rough clothing and a simple diet. Here we see that he would abstain from alcohol. The drinking of alcohol is not banned in the Bible, but excess is condemned. The Christian should never be a drunkard. Excessive alcohol intake is a sad feature of modern times. The ambition of some is the repeated sight of the bottom of a glass. Physicians have expressed great concern about the rising numbers of those affected by liver disease and other long-term effects of alcohol. Continued heavy drinking has damaged many lives, including some Christians. Abstinence is the safest attitude to alcohol. We may not be called to the same rigours as John the Baptist, but we are all called to be distinctively Christian.

Thirdly, we observe that John would be filled with the Holy Spirit from birth or as some translations put it "his mother's womb". The mystery of the sovereignty of God is present in these words. We should always remember that even the youngest children are able to respond to God. We should all seek the guidance and filling of the Holy Spirit in order to be effective in every compartment of our lives.

The Apostle Paul outlined the difference between drink and the Holy Spirit:

And do not be drunk with wine in which is dissipation; (or excess) but be filled with the Spirit, speaking to one another in psalms and hymns and spiritual songs, singing and making melody in your hearts to the Lord. (Ephesians 5: 18-19)

Fourthly, John would make a spiritual impact on the poor and depressed state of Israel. His life and preaching would create an awakening that would prepare people for the ministry of Jesus. The nature of his calling would remind many of the centuries-old achievements of the Prophet Elijah. The Holy Spirit who inspired Elijah's utterances is the Holy Spirit who inspired John the Baptist. He is the same Holy Spirit who is able to inspire and direct us if we allow Him.

John's ministry was to be a paradoxical mixture of fiery preaching, austerity, and joy, culminating in an appalling execution at the hands of a weak and lustful monarch. (Mark 6: 14-29)

Zacharias, the pious, frightened priest, was shocked by what he heard. He and his wife were elderly. They had experienced all those years of disappointment. Doubt immediately clouded his mind. Even Christians of many years can begin to doubt the promises of God. For example, many doubted the promise of a homeland for the Jewish people, but in 1948 that promise was fulfilled. Many have doubted that a large gathering of Jewish people would accept Jesus as their Messiah, but there are increasing Messianic congregations in the land of Israel. Many doubt the literal return or second coming of Jesus, but one day it will happen. Some doubt that Jesus will always be with them and things will work for good. (Romans 8: 28) Because Zacharias doubted, he was made both deaf and dumb for nine months or so till the birth of his son. Let us not forget that God may intervene sometimes painfully in the circumstances of our lives to draw us more closely to Himself. The interview with the angel took longer than the text seems to indicate. What is clear, he returned to his wife, friends and congregation "a non-gibbering wreck."

It is at this point that the qualities of Elizabeth, his wife, become evident. After Zacharias completed his duties, Elizabeth accompanied him home. She, no doubt, cared for him and spoke for him. Having understood her beloved husband's vision, she had faith and believed God would fulfil His promise even in this seemingly impossible situation. She comforted him and, in the course of time, she became pregnant. However, she waited until things became clearer rather than be mocked by the disbelief of her neighbours. This delightful lady remained quiet for five months, knowing that no-one would believe her. There are times when we need wisdom from God to speak openly about what He has done and there are times to be silent. The problem is that we often use this advice to justify our silence.

Luke 1:26-38

26 Now in the sixth month the angel Gabriel was sent by God to a city of Galilee named Nazareth, 27 to a virgin betrothed to a man whose name was Joseph, of the house of David. The virgin's name *was* Mary. 28 And having come in, the angel said to her, "Rejoice, highly favored *one*, the Lord *is* with you; blessed *are* you among women!" 29 But when she saw *him*, she was troubled at his saying, and considered what manner of greeting this was. 30 Then the angel said to her, "Do not be afraid, Mary, for you have found favor with God. 31 And behold, you will conceive in your womb and bring forth a Son, and shall call His name Jesus. 32 He will be great, and will be called the Son of the Highest; and the Lord God will give Him the throne of His father David. 33 And He will reign over the house of Jacob forever, and of His kingdom there will be no end." 34 Then Mary said to the angel, "How can this be, since I do not know a man?" 35 And the angel answered and said to her, "*The* Holy Spirit will come upon you, and the power of the Highest will overshadow you; therefore, also, that Holy One who is to be born will be called the Son of God. 36 Now indeed, Elizabeth your relative has also conceived a son in her old age; and this is now the sixth month for her who was called barren. 37 For with God nothing will be impossible." 38 Then Mary said, "Behold the maidservant of the Lord! Let it be to me according to your word." And the angel departed from her.

Sadly, the words of the greeting given to Mary have divided Christendom for centuries. The old Latin version of the Bible, or Vulgate, gave rise to the prayer phrase, "Hail Mary, full of grace." This, in turn, gave rise to the classic song and beautiful music, "Ave Maria". These words imply that Mary is able in some way to dispense God's love, unmerited favour, and mercy. However, the meaning of the Greek penned by Luke is that Mary herself is not a provider but a receiver of God's grace and mercy. (v. 28) This Latin translation has contributed to the veneration and virtual worship of this amazing and godly woman. The emphasis on and the presence of pictures, statues and prayers to Mary have understandably caused Protestants to reject such claims about her. On the other hand, we should not ignore or cease to admire her role in God's plan of salvation. We can marvel at her obedience to God's call.

This passage speaks to us of a profound mystery that is beyond science and beyond our medical knowledge.

We read that the young teenager Mary was betrothed in marriage. This was a much more legal and formal arrangement than our understanding of engagement. Some have taught that that the virgin birth, or more accurately the virginal conception, of Jesus is an untrue myth. They suggest that it was crafted in order to appeal to Luke's Greco-Roman readers and put Jesus on a par with emperors and other heroes of the ancient world. Instead, we should wonder at the great grace and self-emptying of the Son of God in coming to this earth as a human being.

Paul wrote about Jesus in this way:

Who, being in the form of God, did not consider it robbery to be equal with God, but made Himself of no reputation, taking the form of a bondservant and coming in the likeness of men. And being found in appearance as a man, He humbled Himself and became obedient to the point of death, even the death of a cross. (Philippians 2:6-8)

Mary's future child was described in such terms as to fulfil the Old Testament prophecies in a way far beyond the imagination of those people of first century Israel.

Many had the name 'Jesus' but none matched the meaning of the name as He did. The name 'Jesus' or 'Yeshua' means Saviour. (Matthew 1: 21) He would not give a temporary fix to the problems of a few people, but by His death on a cross would become the Saviour of the world. The name, "Son of the Highest" is a divine title indicating supreme lordship. (v. 32)

We are told about a kingdom over Israel and an everlasting kingdom. (v. 33) There were many new religious movements during the first century. They all faded away, but this one was very different. Few would argue about the influence Jesus has had on the minds and lives of millions of men and women down the centuries.

Jesus' reign over the house of Jacob is as yet only partially fulfilled. Although difficult to imagine, the comparatively few Jews who believe in Yeshua the Messiah will one day become a vast multitude.

Since she was not in a sexual relationship, Mary's puzzlement at the prospect of becoming pregnant was not a sign of doubt as in the case of Zacharias.

We are often bound by our circumstances and have to be reminded time and again, "With God, nothing will be impossible." (v. 37)

Mary accepted her task, and all the possible consequences, dangers and shame. Many of us make supposedly plausible excuses, but few are as equally willing in the service of God.

Luke 1:39-56

39 Now Mary arose in those days and went into the hill country with haste, to a city of Judah, **40** and entered the house of Zacharias and greeted Elizabeth. **41** And it happened, when Elizabeth heard the greeting of Mary, that the babe leaped in her womb; and Elizabeth was filled with the Holy Spirit. **42** Then she spoke out with a loud voice and said, "Blessed *are* you among women, and blessed *is* the fruit of your womb! **43** But why *is* this *granted* to me, that the mother of my Lord should come to me? **44** For indeed, as soon as the voice of your greeting sounded in my ears, the babe leaped in my womb for joy. **45** Blessed *is* she who believed, for there will be a fulfillment of those things which were told her from the Lord." **46** And Mary said: "My soul magnifies the Lord. **47** And my spirit has rejoiced in God my Savior. **48** For He has regarded the lowly state of His maidservant; For behold, henceforth all generations will call me blessed. **49** For He who is mighty has done great things for me, And holy *is* His name. **50** And His mercy *is* on those who fear Him from generation to generation. **51** He has shown strength with His arm; He has scattered *the* proud in the imagination of their hearts. **52** He has put down the mighty from *their* thrones, And exalted *the* lowly. **53** He has filled *the* hungry with good things, And *the* rich He has sent away empty. **54** He has helped His servant Israel, In remembrance of *His* mercy, **55** As He spoke to our fathers, To Abraham and to his seed forever." **56** And Mary remained with her about three months, and returned to her house.

The visit of Mary to Elizabeth's house shows a meeting of kindred spiritual minds in spite of their age difference. They encouraged one another with what God was doing in their lives. It is something Christians can do regularly. We are so often reluctant to talk even with our Christian friends about spiritual matters. It is also possible that Mary had left Nazareth to escape gossip, the charge of fornication and inevitable shame.

This passage contains some important points for our understanding and learning.

Firstly, we notice the mental grasp Elizabeth had about the significance of Mary's coming child. He would not only be the Messiah but also her Lord. We may call Jesus a great figure of history and a great teacher, but do we all crown Him 'Lord'? Are we prepared to be His servants?

Secondly, we are told that the babe Elizabeth was carrying "leaped in her womb for joy." This more than suggests pre-birth personhood. It is sad that many of the world's voters and legislators ignore this important fact when the issue of abortion is discussed.

Thirdly, Elizabeth is the first person in the timeline of the New Testament who is described as "filled with the Holy Spirit". We should recognize that the first person was a woman. Furthermore, the first person to see the risen Lord was a woman. Luke in both his Gospel and Acts showed great respect towards women. We can always point this out when critics charge Christianity as harmful to women.

Fourthly, the eloquence and intelligence of both Mary and Elizabeth in their statements and songs has been considered so unlikely that that certain scholars attribute the verses to a later Christian tradition. Such criticism discounts a number of possibilities.

For one thing, Elizabeth as a wife of a priest and in such a close relationship with her husband would have learnt much about the Hebrew Scriptures. She would have become literate, and able to write Hebrew.

Mary herself was very bright and in the course of three months would have learnt much from her older relative.

Furthermore, some of these academics seem to ignore what the Holy Spirit can do in people's lives. As we shall notice in Luke's writings, the words "full" or "filled with the Holy Spirit" arise on a regular basis.

Mary's song has echoes of the psalms and Hannah's prayer. (1 Samuel 2: 1-10) It begins with Mary's recognition of God's amazing love and grace towards her. God could have chosen a woman connected to the family of an important Jerusalem scribe to be the mother of Jesus. Instead, He chose someone of little means and low social rank. She was the one who would say 'Yes!' and give God all the honour and praise. (vv. 46-49) She goes on to expand the extent of God's grace to the whole world, to every class of person, and to the whole of history. No-one is excluded from the breadth and scope of God's dealings with humanity. (vv. 50-55)

Rulers will be brought down. (v. 52) No dynasty has so far reigned in perpetuity and all empires have come to an end. As a British politician once remarked, "All political careers end in failure." However, we need to pray for all those who exercise power, and all Christians who take part in the political process. In a sense, all who have the right to vote are part of that process.

The poor and insignificant will find meaning and purpose. Their status will be lifted and their hunger satisfied. (v. 53) The proud and rich will be brought down because in eternity their possessions, wealth and power will come to nothing. It is easy to jump to all sorts of political and social conclusions about many aspects of this song. Our understanding of these verses will become clearer as the Gospel and New Testament message unfolds.

The stay with Zacharias and Elizabeth was part of God's preparation for all the challenges and difficulties Mary was about to face on her return to Nazareth. God often prepares His people through some days of prayer, praise, fellowship or just a holiday before a time of service. If we can, let us make the most of our breaks and holidays!

Luke 1:57-80

57 Now Elizabeth's full time came for her to be delivered, and she brought forth a son. 58 When her neighbors and relatives heard how the Lord had shown great mercy to her, they rejoiced with her. 59 So it was, on the eighth day, that they came to circumcise the child; and they would have called him by the name of his father, Zacharias. 60 His mother answered and said, "No; he shall be called John." 61 But they said to her, "There is no one among your relatives who is called by this name." 62 So they made signs to his father—what he would have him called. 63 And he asked for a writing tablet, and wrote, saying, "His name is John." So they all marveled. 64 Immediately his mouth was opened and his tongue *loosed*, and he spoke, praising God. 65 Then fear came on all who dwelt around them; and all these sayings were discussed throughout all the hill country of Judea. 66 And all those who heard *them* kept *them* in their hearts, saying, "What kind of child will this be?" And the hand of the Lord was with him. 67 Now his father Zacharias was filled with the Holy Spirit, and prophesied, saying: 68 "Blessed *is* the Lord God of Israel, For He has visited and redeemed His people, 69 And has raised up a horn of salvation for us in the house of His servant David, 70 As He spoke by the mouth of His holy prophets, Who *have been* since the world began, 71 That we should be saved from our enemies And from the hand of all who hate us, 72 To perform the mercy *promised* to our fathers and to remember His holy covenant, 73 The oath which He swore to our father Abraham: 74 To grant us that we, Being delivered from the hand of our enemies, Might serve Him without fear, 75 In holiness and righteousness before Him all the days of our life. 76 And you, child, will be called the prophet of the Highest; for you will go before the face of the Lord to prepare His ways, 77 To give knowledge of salvation to His people By the remission of their sins, 78 Through the tender mercy of our God, With which the Dayspring from on high has visited us; 79 To give light to those who sit in darkness and the shadow of death, To guide our feet into the way of peace." 80 So the child grew and became strong in spirit, and was in the deserts till the day of his manifestation to Israel.

The birth of John the Baptist was an occasion of great joy and wonder in the surrounding countryside. The aged wife of a priest had given birth, and both mother and child were well. There was some local misunderstanding and chatter about the boy's name. It was customary in those times to give a child a name that was already in the family. When Zacharias wrote on a tablet, "His name is John," he was rewarded with the return of his speech. God is wonderfully patient with His doubting servants even though we may receive painful scars. It is comforting to know that so often we are given a second chance. (Jonah 3: 1)

Time and again, a work for God can go counter to social norms and expectations. Young movements for God frequently meet opposition from quarters where wise advice and encouragement would have been more appropriate.

At an early age, John had something special about him. "The Lord's hand was with him." (v. 66)

Zacharias had changed from a doubting priest to a faithful prophetic voice. Again we read the words, "Filled with the Holy Spirit." Mary had sung about her Lord and Saviour, and Zacharias prophesied about the significance of John the Baptist. Zacharias had written on a tablet about the name of his son. (v. 63) In view of the surrounding fascination concerning the news of John's birth, it is not unreasonable to think that the events, Mary's song, and the words of Zacharias and Elizabeth would have been committed to cherished and valued wooden writing tablets.

Zacharias' song is remarkable in its scope and optimism. The people of Israel longed for a removal of all occupying Roman forces. This downtrodden nation will have all its hopes of freedom, independence and significance realised. (v. 71) Not only that, but there is the spiritual factor of forgiveness of sins, (v.77) and hope in the face of death. (v. 79)

We see an unhindered note of praise. So often our praise is half-hearted and grudging as if our turning up at church is doing God a favour. We may become debilitated by illness, sorrowful in bereavement, shocked by natural disasters and profoundly disappointed by unfulfilled expectations and yet we always have good reason to give God unconditional and unlimited praise. Few can say with Job:

The Lord gave, and the Lord has taken away;
Blessed be the name of the Lord. (Job 1:21)

Zacharias recognised the enormous significance of his newborn child's role, and yet, he knew that John the Baptist and his message would be a preparation for the ministry of Mary's future son, the Lord Jesus.

It is a feature of our world that we project expectations on our children. Self-promotion is seen in secular organizations and sadly also in churches. We need to have a sound estimate of our abilities, not too high and not too low, not proud and not a false humility. Although John the Baptist was up to that time the greatest man who ever lived, (Luke 7:28) he was the one who said of Christ, "He must increase, but I must decrease." (John 3:30)

Finally, it is rarely appreciated that those people and cultures who are without Christ live in darkness. (v. 79) Many think that we can throw off the old values and beliefs of Christianity. In 2008, the slogan put on the sides of London buses was, "There's probably no god. Now stop worrying and enjoy your life." Instead of appreciating they are living in darkness, they consider themselves to be enlightened. However, they tend to ignore the grim state of peoples and nations before the arrival of Christianity to their shores and borders. Even one notable atheist who gave financial support to the above campaign wrote an article admitting that Africa needed Christianity. If it is good for Africa, then it is good for the West!

Christ came into a broken and troubled world. In John's Gospel, Jesus referred to Himself as the "Light of the World." (John 8: 12) It is a sad conclusion that, "men loved darkness rather than light". (John 3: 19) They continue to do so.

The last verse gives us an indication of John's early life in the desert. Some believe that he joined the Essene sect that resided near the Dead Sea at Qumran. Whilst there may be some truth in that, it should be noted that John's ministry was outgoing and to people, whilst the Essenes taught withdrawal and a complete separation from society.

Luke 2:1-20

1 And it came to pass in those days *that* a decree went out from Caesar Augustus that all the world should be registered. 2 This census first took place while Quirinius was governing Syria. 3 So all went to be registered, everyone to his own city. 4 Joseph also went up from Galilee, out of the city of Nazareth, into Judea, to the city of David, which is called Bethlehem, because he was of the house and lineage of David, 5 to be registered with Mary, his betrothed wife, who was with child. 6 So it was, that while they were there, the days were completed for her to be delivered. 7 And she brought forth her firstborn Son, and wrapped Him in swaddling cloths, and laid Him in a manger, because there was no room for them in the inn. 8 Now there were in the same country shepherds living out in the fields, keeping watch over their flock by night. 9 And behold, an angel of the Lord stood before them, and the glory of the Lord shone around them, and they were greatly afraid. 10 Then the angel said to them, "Do not be afraid, for behold, I bring you good tidings of great joy which will be to all people. 11 For there is born to you this day in the city of David a Savior, who is Christ the Lord. 12 And this *will be* the sign to you: You will find a Babe wrapped in swaddling cloths, lying in a manger." 13 And suddenly there was with the angel a multitude of the heavenly host praising God and saying: 14 "Glory to God in the highest, And on earth peace, goodwill toward men!" 15 So it was, when the angels had gone away from them into heaven, that the shepherds said to one another, "Let us now go to Bethlehem and see this thing that has come to pass, which the Lord has made known to us." 16 And they came with haste and found Mary and Joseph, and the Babe lying in a manger. 17 Now when they had seen *Him*, they made widely known the saying which was told them concerning this Child. 18 And all those who heard *it* marveled at those things which were told them by the shepherds. 19 But Mary kept all these things and pondered *them* in her heart. 20 Then the shepherds returned, glorifying and praising God for all the things that they had heard and seen, as it was told them.

The passage anchors the birth of Jesus in history. It was during the reign of Augustus and the governorship of Quirinius. Many have called into question Luke's integrity as a trustworthy historian since the governor ruled 6-9 AD rather than during the reign of Herod. (37 BC-4 BC.) However, there were some contemporary sources which indicated that he also served in some capacity between 6 and 7 BC.

The contrast between the birth and life of Augustus and that of Jesus could not be more pronounced. Augustus was born into a wealthy family. He became dictator and then emperor. He controlled a ruthless military machine and initiated a period of relative peace over a vast Roman empire. He reigned from 27 BC until his death in 14 AD. Because he was the appointed heir of Julius Caesar, he awarded himself the title, "Son of God." His main bequests to us are archaeological ruins and a month named after him.

Jesus was born into relative poverty and obscurity. He had little financial means and no military forces. However, the reign which He initiated goes on to this day. It will know no end. (Isaiah 9: 7) The peace He brings is not political but in the heart and mind of each believer. The Bible describes it as past understanding. (Philippians 4:7)

The birth of Jesus was from a human standpoint, a riskier event than it might have been. The arrival in crowded Bethlehem meant that there was no proper accommodation to be found. Jesus was born in a place normally inhabited by animals, and was laid in a makeshift cradle.

Luke does not emphasise Joseph's role as Matthew does, but his godly character and commitment to both Mary and Jesus shine through the pages.

The news of Jesus' birth was given to a most unlikely group of people, shepherds. The spiritual leaders in the Old Testament were described as shepherds. Sadly, Jeremiah pointed out that they had led the people astray. (Jeremiah 50: 6)

By the time of Jesus, shepherds had a poor social status. They were despised by the upper classes, and considered to be unwashed and ceremonially unclean. They were thought by many to be thieves. It is a massive irony that the angels and their "good tidings" were directed at this fearful group who were little more than beggars. Jesus dignified their trade since they were among His first visitors.

The description and titles given to Jesus by the angels were extraordinary and yet completely true.

Firstly, He is given the title "Saviour". The title is all-encompassing and difficult to take in all at once. Jesus saves us from the penalty of sin, the wrath of God, death, guilt, estrangement, ignorance of God, cultural bondage, despair, stress and meaninglessness. The list hardly stops. We may take many years to even have a small grasp of this reality.

Secondly, He is given the title "Christ" or "Messiah". To first century Israel, their hopes consisted of the expected arrival of a national figure who was to assume kingship over Judah, and deliverance from oppressors as has been noted in Zacharias' song. There was also a hope of a transcendent Messiah from Heaven, both human and divine. Jesus more than fulfilled these yearnings, but in unexpected ways.

Thirdly, He is declared to be "Lord". Elizabeth described Him as her Lord. Jesus is Lord of creation, Lord of life and Lord of the church. "Jesus is Lord" is probably the earliest of Christian confessions. It is a title that brought clashes with authorities in the early days of the church and does so more and more in these present days. If He is our Saviour, then He is also our Lord. The two cannot be divided.

Finally, we notice that the good tidings were accompanied by great joy. (v. 10) We read in the New Testament that in spite of persecutions and hardships, there is wonderful joy when someone becomes a Christian. This joy is both in the believer and in Heaven. (Luke 15:7) The book of Psalms contains the word 'joy' more than fifty times.

It goes a step further than that. We are told that the wise men "rejoiced exceedingly" when they saw the star which led them to Jesus. (Matthew 2:10) When the disciples saw the risen Lord, they were "overjoyed". (John 20:20, NIV)

Many of us receive life's hard knocks and have heartaches that go on day after day, and yet want and dare to say, "The joy of the Lord is my strength." (Nehemiah 8:10)

Luke 2:21-40

21 And when eight days were completed for the circumcision of the Child, His name was called JESUS, the name given by the angel before He was conceived in the womb. 22 Now when the days of her purification according to the law of Moses were completed, they brought Him to Jerusalem to present *Him* to the Lord 23 (as it is written in the law of the Lord, "Every male who opens the womb shall be called holy to the Lord"), 24 and to offer a sacrifice according to what is said in the law of the Lord, "A pair of turtledoves or two young pigeons." 25 And behold, there was a man in Jerusalem whose name *was* Simeon, and this man *was* just and devout, waiting for the Consolation of Israel, and the Holy Spirit was upon him. 26 And it had been revealed to him by the Holy Spirit that he would not see death before he had seen the Lord's Christ. 27 So he came by the Spirit into the temple. And when the parents brought in the Child Jesus, to do for Him according to the custom of the law, 28 he took Him up in his arms and blessed God and said:29 "Lord, now You are letting Your servant depart in peace, According to Your word; 30 For my eyes have seen Your salvation 31 Which You have prepared before the face of all peoples, 32 A light to *bring* revelation to the Gentiles, and the glory of Your people Israel." 33 And Joseph and His mother marveled at those things which were spoken of Him. 34 Then Simeon blessed them, and said to Mary His mother, "Behold, this *Child* is destined for the fall and rising of many in Israel, and for a sign which will be spoken against 35 (yes, a sword will pierce through your own soul also), that the thoughts of many hearts may be revealed." 36 Now there was one, Anna, a prophetess, the daughter of Phanuel, of the tribe of Asher. She was of a great age, and had lived with a husband seven years from her virginity; 37 and this woman *was* a widow of about eighty-four years, who did not depart from the temple, but served *God* with fastings and prayers night and day. 38 And coming in that instant she gave thanks to the Lord, and spoke of Him to all those who looked for redemption in Jerusalem. 39 So when they had performed all things according to the law of the Lord, they returned to Galilee, to their *own* city, Nazareth. 40 And the Child grew and became strong in spirit, filled with wisdom; and the grace of God was upon Him.

We cannot understand Jesus without an appreciation of His Jewish background. He was brought up and lived in accordance with the law.

He was critical of certain extra-traditions evolved by men. His sacrificial death on a cross brought about forgiveness and cancelled various aspects of the law. This included the need for a Temple ceremonial system. Nevertheless, He lived as a Jew.

But when the fullness of the time had come, God sent forth His Son, born of a woman, born under the law, to redeem those who were under the law, that we might receive the adoption as sons. (Galatians 4: 4-5)

The sacrifice of doves or pigeons that Joseph and Mary brought to the Jerusalem temple (v. 24) shows that Jesus was born into a poor family. Jesus knew from experience what it is to have a low income and limited resources. He understood what it was to go without many of the things the prosperous take for granted. He criticised hypocrisy and the misuse of money, but He never blamed anyone for being poor.

Jesus was born into a bleak unforgiving world of darkness, but there were those who longed for the Messiah.

The first encounter was with Simeon who had "the Holy Spirit upon him". (v. 25) We assume from his words that he was elderly. (v. 29) When he saw the babe, he spoke with inspiration. He now had fulfilled his life purpose and was prepared to depart from the scene. He also understood the worldwide significance of Jesus. Jesus would be light in the darkness. This metaphor is repeated in the New Testament and with good reason. Spiritual darkness still inhabits many homes and nations. Some have little desire to throw it off and let in the light. (John 3: 19)

May we also realise that Jesus is not just for a select few, but He extends His invitation to everyone in every street and corner of the world.

Simeon's words came also with a disturbing warning. He pointed out that there would be future opposition and division. The motives of many will be exposed. The rejection and death of Jesus in that very same city, Jerusalem, would also be a cause of great heartache for Mary. (vv. 34-35) There is joy in the service of Christ, but there is also stress and sorrow. Simeon's comments remind us that there are two very important aspects here. The first is the great wonder of what is known as the incarnation, or God becoming human. The second is the redemption or salvation of humanity by Jesus' sacrificial death on the cross. It is worth remembering that the New Testament writers write more about the cross than the incarnation.

The introduction of Anna (v. 36) is poignant. Once again, Luke points us to the importance of women. Not only that, she was elderly. Studies have shown that women over sixty-five provide numerous services and ministries to millions all over the world. The church could not function without them.

Anna had been a widow for around sixty years. She must have been desolate in the early years following the death of her husband. She may have had to bring up a family on her own. Few realise the difficulties and vulnerability of a widow, single or divorcee. Later, in the final stages of His ministry, Jesus warned His hearers to beware of teachers of the law who devour widows' houses. (Luke 20: 46-47) (In modern times, it is some sales people and others who are all too ready to charge extra or skimp over contracts.) However, Anna managed to overcome her early disappointments.

Instead of a descent into self-pity and bitterness, she worshipped and served the Lord in the Temple. She also appears to have had many friends who no doubt treated her as a loving relative. She too recognised the significance of Jesus and spoke naturally to many of the Temple visitors. It is a wonderful gift to talk easily about spiritual matters. It is an unusual gift to speak and avoid the "cringe factor". We should ask God about it repeatedly in prayer.

For John the Baptist, the hand of the Lord was with him. (Ch. 1:66) For Jesus, the grace of God was upon Him. (v. 40) This grace was not the kind of grace that comes to sinners who do not deserve it but as the favour towards Jesus who did. Let us pray that we have these undeserved gifts with us and on us.

Luke 2:41-52

41 His parents went to Jerusalem every year at the Feast of the Passover. **42** And when He was twelve years old, they went up to Jerusalem according to the custom of the feast. **43** When they had finished the days, as they returned, the Boy Jesus lingered behind in Jerusalem. And Joseph and His mother did not know *it;* **44** but supposing Him to have been in the company, they went a day's journey, and sought Him among *their* relatives and acquaintances. **45** So when they did not find Him, they returned to Jerusalem, seeking Him. **46** Now so it was *that* after three days they found Him in the temple, sitting in the midst of the teachers, both listening to them and asking them questions. **47** And all who heard Him were astonished at His understanding and answers. **48** So when they saw Him, they were amazed; and His mother said to Him, "Son, why have You done this to us? Look, Your father and I have sought You anxiously." **49** And He said to them, "Why did you seek Me? Did you not know that I must be about My Father's business?" **50** But they did not understand the statement which He spoke to them. **51** Then He went down with them and came to Nazareth, and was subject to them, but His mother kept all these things in her heart. **52** And Jesus increased in wisdom and stature, and in favor with God and men.

Biographies of politicians, scientists, artists, musicians, industrialists and so on, all have a chapter on the subject's origins, forebears, parents and childhood.

As for Jesus, however, we have precious little information on what are known as "the silent years".

Although we teach that Jesus was born into poverty, we know that Joseph was able to house, clothe, and feed his large family. Every year he financed an eighty-mile family excursion or holiday to Jerusalem in order to celebrate the Passover. They probably went as a group of families. In order to make sure that the slowest went at the same speed as the fastest, the children led the way followed by the women, and then the men.

It was a festival when the Jews remembered their release from slavery and their escape from Egypt centuries before. Every year the priests sacrificed the Passover lambs as a memorial. This ceremony was linked to the forgiveness of sins. The inclusion in Luke's Gospel of the family outing to Jerusalem is particularly poignant, because about twenty years later, Jesus would make His final trip to Jerusalem and be crucified for the forgiveness of sins. He would be the Lamb of God. (John 1: 29)

Whilst Jesus was at the temple, even at twelve years of age, He demonstrated His ability as a respectful learner and even a teacher. Luke makes the fascinating point that Jesus asked the teachers questions, and then everyone was amazed at His understanding and answers! (v.47) We are not told about the subjects of their discussions. They probably centred around the Law or Torah.

We can read all that it is necessary to know of Jesus' teachings from the Gospels and the rest of the New Testament. When Jesus taught, He spoke with a great sense of authority, and not as the religious teachers of His day. (Matthew 7: 29)

The rest of the story could be described as a tension episode with His parents. This could be regarded as something inevitable in the process of growing up, but Jesus was, of course, incapable of acting improperly. At the age of twelve Jewish boys are on the verge of manhood.

In the course of all the family activity and the bustle of the party's return home to Nazareth, they did not know that Jesus was no longer with them. After a day's travel they realized that He had been left behind. Panic set in, and after three days at last they found Him in, guess where, the temple. One cannot have but a little sympathy for Mary and Joseph in their anxiety and complaint. (v.48)

However, it must be stated that both Mary and Joseph should have been aware of the fact that Jesus was indeed the Messiah everyone was hoping for, and in all their inevitable and necessary bustle and business, time should have been set aside for Jesus' discussions with the teachers. Jesus was aware of His unique relationship with God His Father. (v.49)

All children require spiritual input, whether or not they take advantage of it in later life. Having brought up a family, I am reluctant to give advice on parenting. However, from this passage we learn the importance of giving proper attention to the spiritual side of our humanity.

Afterwards, we read that Jesus grew in wisdom and stature, and in favour with God and men. No doubt He earned a living for His family in the building trade. He would have seen the activities of farmers, fishermen, merchants, soldiers and religious teachers. All these would be part of His later ministry. A century or so ago an American president stated that he thought that a knowledge of the Bible was more important than a college education.

For the second time in Luke we read that Mary treasured these things in her heart. (v.51 and 2:19) This indicates that she would have talked about them to selected individuals. If she lived to a great age, she might even have had discussions with Luke himself.

Luke 3:1-6

1 Now in the fifteenth year of the reign of Tiberius Caesar, Pontius Pilate being governor of Judea, Herod being tetrarch of Galilee, his brother Philip tetrarch of Iturea and the region of Trachonitis, and Lysanias tetrarch of Abilene, 2 while Annas and Caiaphas were high priests, the word of God came to John the son of Zacharias in the wilderness. 3 And he went into all the region around the Jordan, preaching a baptism of repentance for the remission of sins, 4 as it is written in the book of the words of Isaiah the prophet, saying: "The voice of one crying in the wilderness: 'Prepare the way of the LORD; Make His paths straight. 5 Every valley shall be filled And every mountain and hill brought low; The crooked places shall be made straight And the rough ways smooth; 6 And all flesh shall see the salvation of God.'"

Once again Luke described actions that were rooted in history. It was a common practice in the ancient world to link events to the years of emperors and governors. We can estimate that John the Baptist's ministry began between 25 and 29 AD.

John came out of his solitary existence and felt the call of God to preach in the desert around the Jordan River of all places. In Matthew's Gospel we are told about the rough nature of John's clothing and the simplicity of his diet. (Matthew 3:4)

He began with a message of repentance. Preachers and the rest of us would do well if services, meetings and prayers contained words about repentance. In some places of worship, repentance is easily forgotten and hardly mentioned. Jesus and the apostles preached repentance. It has a particular place in the Lord's Prayer (Luke 11:4).

True repentance is associated with apology, and saying "Sorry!" directed to God. It is combined with a determination to put things right and not repeat whatever we have thought, said or done. It comes from a sense of God speaking to our consciences.

The Psalmist put it in a heart-felt prayer as follows:

Blot out my transgressions.
Wash me thoroughly from my iniquity,
And cleanse me from my sin.
For I acknowledge my transgressions,
And my sin is always before me.
Against You, You only, have I sinned,
And done this evil in Your sight-
That You may be found just when You speak,
And blameless when You judge. (Psalm 51: 1-4)

True repentance leads to forgiveness. Forgiveness is a specifically Judeo-Christian concept. God promises to forgive, no ifs no buts. It is as if the situation never happened.

Worldly guilt leads to self-blame and a downward spiral of repeated self-loathing. A godly sense of guilt and repentance leads to forgiveness and restoration. That is why John talked about a baptism of repentance leading to remission or forgiveness of sins. Jesus, by His death on the cross, bore the penalty and allows forgiveness to happen. Repentance is the way of access.

This is a crucial topic, and we become stunted Christians if we do not have a sufficient understanding. It is easy to go on accusing ourselves about the past when God has already forgiven us. It is God who convicts of sin. (John 16: 8) It is Satan who is described as the accuser of the brethren. (Revelation 12: 10)

The Jewish people knew that there was something wrong with the world, something wrong with their country and something wrong with themselves. With notable exceptions, modern, affluent people believe the first two but insist that they themselves are all right. They may make bad choices occasionally but in the main they are pretty decent and law-abiding, but all too many are in a state of spiritual darkness.

John challenged his hearers to an act usually reserved for "dirty Gentiles" who became Jews. These were known as proselytes. In the Old Testament, the prophet Elisha advised Naaman the Syrian army commander, a Gentile, to go and wash in Jordan seven times before he could be cleansed of his leprosy. (2 Kings 5:10)

The symbolism is striking. The first century Jews left the bustle, dirt and corruption of Jerusalem and other towns, and went out to the quiet of the desert. They heard the message, pondered its content, received a baptismal wash and returned cleansed to their homes.

If people were going to be truly ready for the Messiah they had to know a baptism of repentance. For us, baptism symbolises the death of my old self so that my new self in Christ Jesus can emerge into a new life. (Romans 6: 3-4) Many regard baptism as a chance to welcome a baby into the world and a social get-together. Others go through the ritual in order to gain a label of decency. Baptism is of no value unless it accompanied with a good-bye to the old life, a desire for a new birth, and faith in Christ.

Finally, Luke quoted Isaiah. (Isaiah 40: 3-5) This put John's ministry into the context of the Old Testament. Even here, the quote from Isaiah enlarges the message to include all of humanity. (v.6) (Isaiah 52: 10)

Luke 3:7-20

7 Then he said to the multitudes that came out to be baptized by him, "Brood of vipers! Who warned you to flee from the wrath to come? **8** Therefore bear fruits worthy of repentance, and do not begin to say to yourselves, 'We have Abraham as *our* father.' For I say to you that God is able to raise up children to Abraham from these stones. **9** And even now the ax is laid to the root of the trees. Therefore every tree which does not bear good fruit is cut down and thrown into the fire." **10** So the people asked him, saying, "What shall we do then?" **11** He answered and said to them, "He who has two tunics, let him give to him who has none; and he who has food, let him do likewise." **12** Then tax collectors also came to be baptized, and said to him, "Teacher, what shall we do?" **13** And he said to them, "Collect no more than what is appointed for you." **14** Likewise the soldiers asked him, saying, "And what shall we do?" So he said to them, "Do not intimidate anyone or accuse falsely, and be content with your wages." **15** Now as the people were in expectation, and all reasoned in their hearts about John, whether he was the Christ *or* not, **16** John answered, saying to all, "I indeed baptize you with water; but One mightier than I is coming, whose sandal strap I am not worthy to loose. He will baptize you with the Holy Spirit and fire. **17** His winnowing fan *is* in His hand, and He will thoroughly clean out His threshing floor, and gather the wheat into His barn; but the chaff He will burn with unquenchable fire." **18** And with many other exhortations he preached to the people. **19** But Herod the tetrarch, being rebuked by him concerning Herodias, his brother Philip's wife, and for all the evils which Herod had done, **20** also added this, above all, that he shut John up in prison.

"Brood of vipers! Who warned you to flee from the wrath to come?" (v.7) The proclamation will come as a shock to those who have a view of God as a benign Father Christmas, or avuncular overseer whose ultimate job is to agree with us. Let us do what we want and not be overly concerned with wrong!

John in his tough direct way pointed out that there is a judgment and that we are accountable. Our surprise should not be that God is a God of judgment but that He is also full of mercy, kindness and forgiveness. Preachers need to get the balance right. We do no favours to anyone if judgment is omitted from the Gospel message. We also do a grave disservice if God's love, salvation, and understanding of our circumstances are not given sufficient emphasis.

In those days, many in the crowds rested on their laurels and felt that their ancestry was sufficient to bring about God's favour. (v. 8) We tend to seek assurance for ourselves by our background and culture. That is an insecure foundation when dealing with eternal matters. John said that we all need to change our attitude to God and everyone we meet. (v.11)

Two connected groups of despised people are then mentioned. Even they made the journey to Jordan. The respectable regarded them with utter contempt. The tax collectors were collaborators with the hated Romans. They collected money for the Romans and charged extra for themselves. The soldiers enforced that system.

What should they do? Should they stop or should they continue?

It is interesting that John did not tell them to stop but to be just and honest. We do not like to pay tax but it is necessary to maintain a nation. Soldiers are needed, and if used correctly, can defend the weak and uphold peace and order in the world.

John's impact was considerable and was also noted by the Jewish historian Josephus. It was natural to wonder if John could possibly be the promised Messiah. It would have been tempting for John to assume a mantle of great importance. He was enjoying success. Thousands flocked to hear him. It was a heady mixture that has been repeated down the centuries, and many have fallen for it. Not so with John, he wanted to give proper honour to the true Messiah, and diminish his own ministry. To remove someone's sandal was a task given to the lowest of servants. To be unworthy of even that shows John the Baptist's profound obedience to God's will and plan.

John's next comments are as challenging as they are striking. (v. 16)

Baptism with fire refers to a number of issues, which are of deep significance.

Fire, in the context of the passage, makes a reference to judgment in general and the final judgment in particular.

The book of 2 Peter makes the point that everything will be destroyed by fire. Astrophysicists predict that in the far distant future such a thing will happen to the earth and the rest of the solar system. The point is, that if that indeed is the final outcome, then we ought to live God-centred lives, fit for a new heaven and a new earth. (2 Peter 3: 10-13)

Secondly, we read in Acts about the coming of the Holy Spirit on the early church as tongues of fire on each individual. (Acts 2: 3) This was symbolic of the power of God to enable them to speak in languages about God's wonderful works.

God's gift of the Holy Spirit to each believer should enliven each one to be on fire with the mission and love of God.

One translation of 1 Thessalonians 5: 19 is, "Do not put out the Spirit's fire." (NIV) There are many Christians who when faced with routine, disappointments and tragedy quench the Holy Spirit's influence on their lives. They become stale and ineffective.

It is a good regular request to pray that we be filled with the fire of God's love. It is a tragedy when Christians lose their sparkle and become bound by habit and perfunctory tedium.

Even John with all his preaching about judgment and doom spoke about the good news of a coming Messiah.

As the ministry of Jesus increased, John still spoke his courageous message. When he rebuked Herod Antipas for his adulterous affair with his brother's wife, he suffered imprisonment and subsequent beheading.

Luke 3:21-38

21 When all the people were baptized, it came to pass that Jesus also was baptized; and while He prayed, the heaven was opened. **22** And the Holy Spirit descended in bodily form like a dove upon Him, and a voice came from heaven which said, "You are My beloved Son; in You I am well pleased." **23** Now Jesus Himself began *His ministry at* about thirty years of age, being (as was supposed) *the* son of Joseph, *the son* of Heli, **24** *the son* of Matthat, *the son* of Levi, *the son* of Melchi, *the son* of Janna, *the son* of Joseph, **25** *the son* of Mattathiah, *the son* of Amos, *the son* of Nahum, *the son* of Esli, *the son* of Naggai, **26** *the son* of Maath, *the son* of Mattathiah, *the son* of Semei, *the son* of Joseph, *the son* of Judah, **27** *the son* of Joannas, *the son* of Rhesa, *the son* of Zerubbabel, *the son* of Shealtiel, *the son* of Neri, **28** *the son* of Melchi, *the son* of Addi, *the son* of Cosam, *the son* of Elmodam, *the son* of Er, **29** *the son* of Jose, *the son* of Eliezer, *the son* of Jorim, *the son* of Matthat, *the son* of Levi, **30** *the son* of Simeon, *the son* of Judah, *the son* of Joseph, *the son* of Jonan, *the son* of Eliakim, **31** *the son* of Melea, *the son* of Menan, *the son* of Mattathah, *the son* of Nathan, *the son* of David, **32** *the son* of Jesse, *the son* of Obed, *the son* of Boaz, *the son* of Salmon, *the son* of Nahshon, **33** *the son* of Amminadab, *the son* of Ram, *the son* of Hezron, *the son* of Perez, *the son* of Judah, **34** *the son* of Jacob, *the son* of Isaac, *the son* of Abraham, *the son* of Terah, *the son* of Nahor, **35** *the son* of Serug, *the son* of Reu, *the son* of Peleg, *the son* of Eber, *the son* of Shelah, **36** *the son* of Cainan, *the son* of Arphaxad, *the son* of Shem, *the son* of Noah, *the son* of Lamech, **37** *the son* of Methuselah, *the son* of Enoch, *the son* of Jared, *the son* of Mahalalel, *the son* of Cainan, **38** *the son* of Enosh, *the son* of Seth, *the son* of Adam, *the son* of God.

The baptism of Jesus is as wonderful as it was unlikely. If anyone did not need baptism, it was Jesus. He did not sin. He did not need to repent. Yet in His humility, He identified Himself with each one of us, in His process of redemption for humanity. He took on our mantle and went to the cross to satisfy the wrath of God, bare our sins, and bring salvation and forgiveness.

In this incident we see all three persons of the Trinity acting together in one purpose.

The Father sent the Holy Spirit in a bodily form like a dove and demonstrated the relationship that Jesus had throughout His life. Jesus and the Holy Spirit were inseparable and Jesus always did those things which pleased His Father.

"You are My beloved Son, in You I am well pleased. " (v.22) was true then as it was in all of His life. The Holy Spirit was with Him in His temptations, ministry, prayers, healings, that awful time in the Garden of Gethsemane, (Luke 22: 39-46) and His road to the cross. When we become Christians, we ask Christ into our lives. We also receive the Holy Spirit. This was not a general phenomenon before Jesus came in His earthly form. Indwelling of the Holy Spirit came to all true believers after His death and resurrection and the day of Pentecost:

Then Peter said to them, "Repent, and let every one of you be baptized in the name of Jesus Christ for the remission of sins; and you shall receive the gift of the Holy Spirit. For the promise is to you and your children, and to all who are afar off, as many as the Lord our God will call." (Acts 2: 38-39)

On conversion, we have the greatest of privileges, the indwelling of the Holy Spirit. However, unlike Jesus, who never grieved the Holy Spirit, we can. As well as quenching or putting out the Sprit's fire, we can grieve the Holy Spirit. (Isaiah 63: 10) We grieve the Holy Spirit by purposefully neglecting Jesus and by disobedience to God's Word. It occurs when we live like the world, lie, steal, curse or become embittered. We grieve Him when we disrespect or pour scorn on some of God's people. Sadly, even Christians can abuse and persecute fellow Christians. Kindness, compassion and forgiveness are in agreement with the will of Christ. (Ephesians 4: 32)

The Apostle Paul warns us, "And do not grieve the Holy Spirit of God, by whom you were sealed for the day of redemption." (Ephesians 4:30) When we grieve the Holy Spirit continually, His promptings, joy and peace become less clear and less frequent. The prayer of the Psalmist was:

Create in me a clean heart, O God, And renew a steadfast spirit within me. Do not cast me away from Your presence And do not take Your Holy Spirit from me. Restore to me the joy of Your salvation, And uphold me by Your generous Spirit. (Psalm 51: 10-12)

In our day, although the Holy Spirit cannot be taken away from a believer, the believer can lose the joy of salvation.

Genealogies and family trees receive more interest than they did. Even so, few know much about the names and lives of their forebears beyond their grandparents. In those days and even in many parts of today's world, they are of vital importance for people to understand who they are, where they come from and their position in society.

Verses 23 to 30 consist of a long list of Jesus' ancestors. The Apostle Paul urges us not to become bogged down and obsessed by disputes about the technicalities of endless genealogies. (I Timothy 1: 4) It does not mean that we should ignore them altogether. Critics of Jesus later thought of all sorts of reasons to deny the person and messiahship of Jesus. There were those who disputed the reality of His humanity. From this list we see that Jesus is a real person, son of David, son of Abraham and the Son of God. The story of Jesus did not come about by a series of concocted fables that by some vague and ill-defined process evolved into the Gospel account. He was a real person who lived in real places in the context of real history.

Luke 4:1-8

1 Then Jesus, being filled with the Holy Spirit, returned from the Jordan and was led by the Spirit into the wilderness, 2 being tempted for forty days by the devil. And in those days He ate nothing, and afterward, when they had ended, He was hungry. 3 And the devil said to Him, "If You are the Son of God, command this stone to become bread." 4 But Jesus answered him, saying, "It is written, 'Man shall not live by bread alone, but by every word of God.'" 5 Then the devil, taking Him up on a high mountain, showed Him all the kingdoms of the world in a moment of time. 6 And the devil said to Him, "All this authority I will give You, and their glory; for *this* has been delivered to me, and I give it to whomever I wish. 7 Therefore, if You will worship before me, all will be Yours." 8 And Jesus answered and said to him, "Get behind Me, Satan! For it is written, 'You shall worship the Lord your God, and Him only you shall serve.' "

Often, when speakers talk on the above verses, they move very quickly onto the temptations in the wilderness, and give little mention to the words in the first verse, 'Jesus, being filled with the Holy Spirit'.

The New Testament describes a number of people who were full of the Holy Spirit. Here we have Jesus. We have read already about Elizabeth and that her son John the Baptist was described as a man full of the Holy Spirit from his mother's womb. (Luke 1: 15) At the day of Pentecost, Peter and the other believers are noted to be full of the Holy Spirit. (Acts 2: 4) The requirement for being one of the seven deacons, whose chief function was to be administration, is that they should be men, 'full of the Holy Spirit'. (Acts 6: 3) Stephen in the moments before his martyrdom was '"full of the Holy Spirit". (Acts 7: 55)

Since these individuals were "full of the Holy Spirit", this can and should be part of every Christian's life.

It is at this point that I would like to mention two negatives. First of all, being full of the Holy Spirit is not to promote a crude kind of personal projection, as might be seen in a celebrity culture. "Hey guys, look at me!" Jesus was invited by Satan to do just that, but He rejected it. Although His signs and miracles demonstrated His divinity, He did not parade it, as might a showman. Secondly, in the Bible, no one ever said, "I am full of the Holy Spirit." They may have been aware of something but it was others who noticed and commented. God wants you to live a life, so that others might notice that you have been with Jesus. It is as if we should have God's fingerprints all over us.

The primary purpose of the Holy Spirit within us is not to make us feel good, or joyful, but something far more basic. He is present in order to glorify God. For John the Baptist, it was to enable him to be a fearless prophet-preacher, and the enduring of a long imprisonment, culminating in his execution. Peter was full of the Holy Spirit, when he faced and answered boldly, cross-examination in court. (Acts 4: 8-13) The gift was given to the deacons so that they could show compassion and competence in the early church's system of caring for the needs of widows. (Acts 6: 3) Stephen was full of the Holy Spirit in order to face with wonderful serenity, death by stoning, accompanied by prayer for those who stoned him. (Acts 7: 55) To the Ephesians, it is the area of worship, relationships in marriage, the family, home and work. (Ephesians 5: 18 - 6: 9)

Jesus was led by the Spirit into the wilderness. Some people, at critical points in their lives, go away to prepare themselves. We may think that by going into the mountains or countryside we will be free of distractions and feel close to God. This is not necessarily the case. It can be a time when we are most at risk of getting our priorities and motives confused. Such was the nature of the temptations that Jesus had to face. Luke tells us that these temptations came when He was hungry, a time when we are most vulnerable.

At first, Satan tempted Jesus to exploit His position as God's Son, doubt His Father's providing care, and turn stones into bread. Such action would have satiated His hunger, and on a wider scale would have brought Him great political popularity. It would have enhanced on every level His claim to be Israel's Messiah. Jesus replied, by quoting Scripture, "Man does not live by bread alone." (Deuteronomy 8: 3) Jesus demonstrated His utter dependence on His Father's care.

In the second temptation, Jesus was tempted to be worldly. Jesus was taken to a high vantage point where humanly speaking He could probably see as far as the Mediterranean Sea. In fact, He experienced a vision of all the kingdoms of the Earth. He was told that all this belonged to Satan. In one sense this is true. So many people are resistant to God's rule and Kingdom. But really, it was a lie. The world is God's world and is ultimately subject to His just and gentle rule. Jesus had the power and brilliance to gain political control and live, as King Herod did, in sumptuous palaces, with a military arm as Muhammad had and have countless servants just like a Roman emperor. Instead, He ate the poor man's food, wore the poor man's clothes and died a criminal's death in order to save and give forgiveness to those who would believe in Him. Jesus was tempted to exploit His talents for selfish and worldly ends. He refused, again quoting Scripture, 'It is written: "You shall worship the Lord your God and Him only shall you serve." (From Deuteronomy 6: 13)

Luke 4:9-13

9 Then he brought Him to Jerusalem, set Him on the pinnacle of the temple, and said to Him, "If You are the Son of God, throw Yourself down from here. **10** For it is written: 'He shall give His angels charge over you, To keep you,' **11** and, 'In *their* hands they shall bear you up, Lest you dash your foot against a stone.'" **12** And Jesus answered and said to him, "It has been said, 'You shall not tempt the LORD your God.' " **13** Now when the devil had ended every temptation, he departed from Him until an opportune time.

The third temptation is strange because we are told that Jesus intersperses His time in the wilderness with a trip to the highest point of the Jerusalem temple. Here, He is tempted to presume on God's care. In inviting Jesus to throw Himself off the top of the pinnacle, Satan tempted Jesus to relinquish His humanity. Jesus took on our humanity, so as to be tempted as we are, yet be without sin, to be obedient even to the point of death on a cross.

The devil, cynically quoted a Psalm in order to bolster his cause. This Psalm is frequently a comfort to believers in facing a future possibly dangerous task, but in this case, its meaning is distorted by Satan:

He shall give His angels charge over you, To keep you; in their hands they shall bear you up, Lest you dash your foot against a stone. (Psalm 91; 11-12)

The spectacle of a successful stunt, seen and witnessed by thousands of residents and visitors to Jerusalem would have the probability of attracting crowds of adherents in an instant. Jesus, however, wishes to have people who have transformed and faithful lives, and not dependent on outrageous gimmicks.

Jesus replied, giving a correct application of Scripture, "You shall not tempt the LORD your God." (Deuteronomy 6: 16)

Scripture describes Satan as the Father of all lies (John 8: 44) and the accuser of the brethren. (Revelation 12: 10) This passage demonstrates the first part particularly well.

It is possible to be deceived by misquoting, or the erroneous use of Scripture. The teaching and application of the so-called prosperity gospel is a good if cruel example. The promise of riches and abundant finances is a delusion, which false teachers often peddle to gain money for themselves. These men are to be found on certain radio and TV stations. A number of them have been shown to be the subjects of scandal and guilty of fraud, but still have the calculating ability to reinvent themselves, so that they can return to the microphone and the TV screen. Yes, we do have biblical promises that God cares for those who put their trust in Him, but frequently we still have to work hard as Joseph and Jesus did in order to provide for our families and ourselves. On countless occasions, the apostles and subsequent servants of Christ, both women and men, have faced severe hardship and suffering for the sake of the Gospel and God's kingdom.

Jesus quoted and applied Scripture in a correct way. Being full of the Holy Spirit, He had a memory bank of those passages from the Hebrew Bible, which in turn had been inspired by the very same Holy Spirit. It is important for all of us to read the Bible daily in order to gain such a memory bank.

A few years ago, I was seriously ill, to the extent that I was prevented from continuing my career as an orthopaedic surgeon. Although it was not a cancer, it was equally dangerous, and required two courses of chemotherapy. I was hardly able to walk down the street and could only manage to concentrate on a mere paragraph of a book or newspaper. However, it was at that point I was able to draw on a memory of past Bible reading. That reading had been over previous decades, and not always at times when I felt like it. Nevertheless, memories of past verses came to mind and were nearly always relevant for the trials of that day. These were of great comfort and strength, and I was very grateful to Christian teachers and friends from my youth who had commended and urged the discipline of daily Bible reading. When we are in the transit lounge of life and death, these are the words and things that become of great importance.

In the case of temptation, Scripture can be used to recognise and resist not only temptation, but also the devil himself. Paul in his letter to the Ephesians talks about the Christian's armour. The shield of faith is there to resist the "fiery darts of the wicked one", (Ephesians 6: 16) or what could be described as cruel accusations and temptations. Furthermore, we are entitled to take up the sword of the Spirit, which is the word of God. (Ephesians 6: 17) If Jesus was familiar with the Scriptures, we should do our best to be as knowledgeable as we can.

Luke 4:14-22

14 Then Jesus returned in the power of the Spirit to Galilee, and news of Him went out through all the surrounding region. **15** And He taught in their synagogues, being glorified by all. **16** So He came to Nazareth, where He had been brought up. And as His custom was, He went into the synagogue on the Sabbath day, and stood up to read. **17** And He was handed the book of the prophet Isaiah. And when He had opened the book, He found the place where it was written: **18** "The Spirit of the Lord *is* upon Me, because He has anointed Me to preach the gospel to *the* poor; He has sent Me to heal the brokenhearted, To proclaim liberty to *the* captives And recovery of sight to *the* blind, To set at liberty those who are oppressed; **19** To proclaim the acceptable year of the Lord." **20** Then He closed the book, and gave *it* back to the attendant and sat down. And the eyes of all who were in the synagogue were fixed on Him. **21** And He began to say to them, "Today this Scripture is fulfilled in your hearing." **22** So all bore witness to Him, and marveled at the gracious words which proceeded out of His mouth. And they said, "Is this not Joseph's son?"

After the temptations, we are told that Jesus retuned to Galilee in the power of the Spirit. It is clear that Luke is saying that the victory over Satan and temptation led to a change of gear, and now Jesus is ready for His ministry and destiny. Have you ever seen photos of the Sea of Galilee, or had the opportunity to visit? It is a most beautiful place. At that time, it was a place of political unrest and agitation.

Jesus was a teacher rabbi, a status for which Jesus would have had some preparation, although probably not along the usual pathway. In first century Israel, rabbis were different from those of today. They were not necessarily linked to a particular synagogue or religious establishment. They were men who attracted around them schools of followers, and taught in the manner of the old sages. It was quite customary to speak using the model of the parable, just as Jesus did. They interpreted the Hebrew Scriptures, or what we usually call the Old Testament in their own particularly personal or idiosyncratic way.

From this story, we know that Jesus was literate, and could read Hebrew. Having lived in Nazareth, which was at the crossroads of a cosmopolitan trade route, it is likely that He spoke Greek, and possibly Latin. Young Jewish men learnt the first five books of the Bible and much of the subsequent text. Jesus would have known all of the Old Testament by heart. One interesting, and striking point is that because of the importance of reading and knowledge of the Scriptures, it is likely that the Jews were the most literate people in the ancient world.

Jesus' early ministry and teaching was received with praise and astonishment. Then came a key test for any teacher, a return to the town of their childhood and youth. Jesus went to the place of worship on the Sabbath day, as was His custom. It is a habit that we would do well to copy. If Jesus found it necessary, so should we praise the Lord in the Lord's house on the Lord's Day, to be with the Lord's people and to receive the Lord's teaching.

There was a great sense of expectation and anticipation when Jesus was handed the scroll containing the writings of the prophet Isaiah. He took part of Isaiah 61 and used it as a keynote for His following sermon. We do not know the full content of that sermon. However, the reaction to it was dramatic and hostile.

From our perspective, we can look at the passage, which Jesus read, and note a number of interpretations.

Firstly, we can say that the people in this passage that are described as poor are the Jews who regarded themselves as the 'poor of Israel'. They were not an independent nation, but under the yoke of a succession of occupying powers. The current ones were the pagan Romans. They enforced their rule by means of a ruthless oppression, of which execution by crucifixion was the most powerful and cruel of symbols. This was accompanied by a crippling system of taxation, administered by that most hated wealthy and corrupt group, the tax collectors. It was as if the Jews were still in a state of exile. So any introduction on this topic would have been politically dangerous, provocative, and threatening to the governing authorities.

A second interpretation has been given impetus by certain South American writers, and has gained influence in many parts of the world. Many in South America suffer grinding poverty, with its associated poor social conditions, lack of reasonable healthcare, and sparse educational opportunities. This is in the presence of large multi-national companies and autocratic dictatorships, which have exploited their populations. So these writers see Jesus' teaching in terms of a transfer of wealth and power to those who are the exploited, poor and marginalised. There is much to commend this view, and we would all do well to consider the causes as well as the alleviation of poverty.

Nevertheless, in view of Jesus' subsequent teaching, it can be pointed out that there is still much more to His teaching, which I think is even more profound than a socio-political manifesto. Jesus usually came under criticism when He challenged the complacent status of His hearers. One of His greatest challenges to them and to us is the exposure of the widely held notion that we are alright. "I may have some faults but I am as good as anyone else, and not as bad as some people I could mention. I am going to live my life my way, and it is up to God, if He is there, to support me in that process."

The first century inhabitants of Israel believed that the world was divided into two types of people, Jew and Gentile. They as the former were descendants of Abraham, the objects of God's promises and covenants, and custodians of the Law, given to them by God through Moses. They believed profoundly, that as God's chosen people they had an innate superiority over all others, and this belief paraded itself in the form of a legalistic self-righteousness. Although this is a simple understanding, it can be seen that both attitudes are similar in their self-understanding, and their self-righteousness.

It may not be clear from an initial reading, who the poor, the prisoners, the blind and the oppressed are. However, from the general ministry and other words and teachings of Jesus, the poor are not necessarily, those who are short of cash, but those who are poor in spirit who know and acknowledge their desperate need of God. In fact they are not just alright, or secure because they happen to have been born under particular circumstances but are in a state of separation, eternal separation, from God. Prisoners are not only those who are incarcerated subjects of a penal system, but also those who are bound up by their own self-satisfied attitudes, and social addictions. The blind are those who are blind to their own wrongdoings. The oppressed are those who are, perhaps even unwittingly, bound up and polluted by sin and Godless attitudes.

In fact, Jesus is referring to everyone who has lived upon this planet. This realization, when it comes, is a shocking conclusion, which most would regard as completely absurd. When I was a young surgeon in training, I would look up to and admire my mentors as men of towering ability, knowledge and integrity, whose skill I was trying to emulate. Could Jesus be referring to these types of persons too?

The fact is, although these people have great natural gifts, and the world needs such people to function as in any kind of civilization, these too are included in Jesus' words. That's the most striking and alarming thing about them. No matter who we are, we are all included!

Jesus gives us the resolution and the remedy. In Matthew's gospel He states:

"Come to Me, all you who labor and are heavy laden, and I will give you rest. Take My yoke upon you and learn from Me, for I am gentle and lowly in heart, and you will find rest for your souls. For My yoke is easy and My burden is light." (Matthew 11: 28- 30)

So there it is, in the most straightforward and winsome language. Recognise our need and say 'Yes!' to His invitation. Jesus became poor for us so that we could become rich. He was oppressed, ridiculed and ultimately He died on a cross to receive the curse and the punishment we deserve, so that we might receive total forgiveness. No-one is outside His remit.

There was a man from Hull, a city on our Eastern coast. He was from a family with a violent father. He spent his time as a seaman and a fisherman. However, he became involved in crime, and was sent to prison for burglary. During his time, near here, he started going to the prison chapel, and he also read a copy of the Bible. This was the beginning of a profound change in his outlook and attitude. He confessed his whole life of wrongdoing, underwent a real, not temporary, change of heart and mind, committed his life to Christ and experienced God's forgiveness.

Following release from prison, he studied for a degree, and later became, guess what, a prison chaplain. He now works in South America, running orphanages, and planting churches.

Here is a man who demonstrates vividly the type of person Jesus was describing. He was a prisoner. He was released ultimately from a physical prison, part of the justice system. Moreover, he was released from his mental and spiritual prison. The one who said 'No!' to God became the one who said 'Yes!'. The one who sought to rob others, now is one who gives to others. This is a change that only Jesus can bring about.

The question we have to ask is, am I a prisoner in some or even a similar way? Although we may not have gone to a physical prison, Christ wants us to admit that without Him, we are in a spiritual and mental one, and we need to make similar confessions and commitments as the man I have described. Let's thank God for Christ's and the Bible's wonderful and searching diagnosis of the human condition; poor, imprisoned, blind and oppressed. Even more wonderful is recovery of sight, and His all-sufficient remedy and release.

Luke 4:23-30

23 He said to them, "You will surely say this proverb to Me, 'Physician, heal yourself! Whatever we have heard done in Capernaum, do also here in Your country.'" **24** Then He said, "Assuredly, I say to you, no prophet is accepted in his own country. **25** But I tell you truly, many widows were in Israel in the days of Elijah, when the heaven was shut up three years and six months, and there was a great famine throughout all the land; **26** but to none of them was Elijah sent except to Zarephath, *in the region* of Sidon, to a woman *who was* a widow. **27** And many lepers were in Israel in the time of Elisha the prophet, and none of them was cleansed except Naaman the Syrian." **28** So all those in the synagogue, when they heard these things, were filled with wrath, **29** and rose up and thrust Him out of the city; and they led Him to the brow of the hill on which their city was built, that they might throw Him down over the cliff. **30** Then passing through the midst of them, He went His way.

This passage teaches us a number of things about human nature at its worst. We like to think that people are basically good and that with a sound education they will become constructive citizens. Although we are made in God's image, because of the Fall, there is an inbuilt bias in all of us to do wrong. A toddler does not have to be taught to be selfish or how to tell lies. We resist the verdict of Scripture:

The heart is deceitful above all things, And desperately wicked; Who can know it. (Jeremiah 17:9)

And:

This is the condemnation, that the light has come into the world, and men loved darkness rather than light, because their deeds were evil. (John 3: 19)

Firstly, we see that human beings are fickle. They knew Jesus from the past. He grew up in Nazareth and was one of them. They were surprised and admired His wonderful and gracious words. However, the admiration soon turned to scorn and hatred. Although there is much human kindness in the world, human beings are often swayed by the mind-set of those around them. This is even to the extent of a rapid change from positive thoughts about someone to grossly negative ones. The point that Jesus made about God's kindness to Gentiles, namely Naaman the Syrian and the widow of Zarephath, outraged His hearers. If Jesus could have any claim to be a Messiah then He would revive Israel and crush their enemies. To give Gentiles any special place in God's provision was just too much!

Secondly, human beings are manipulative. They have a tendency to use Christ to favour their own ends. He is treated like a lucky charm. "He is there to give me strength. Jesus should give me what I want." The Nazareth congregation had heard of Jesus' works and miracles elsewhere. Why could not they have a share of the action? It was His job to heal and He owed it to His hometown residents.

There are many who are attracted to Jesus, but on condition that He makes them healthy and happy, provides a good job and plenty of money, a good spouse and home. Now, we may have some or all of these things. Nevertheless, when we become Christians, we are committed servants whatever the cost. He promises forgiveness and eternal life. He does not promise a life of ease and worldly success. We may have to endure hardship and suffering like so many of God's people in numerous parts of the world today.

Many fall away when disappointments and trials arise.

Thirdly, human beings can be violent and murderous. We often hear the phrase that some people behaved like animals. In fact, there is no more violent species on earth than human beings. We are capable of great heights and also of great depths. There were a number of assassination attempts or intents on Jesus' life. The first was described by Matthew, (Matthew 2: 13-16) and the second was described in this passage. However, in spite of the frenzy and hate, Jesus walked through the crowd.

So far, in Luke's Gospel, we have seen Jesus as a wonderful teacher with power of words and ideas. He has healed people. Here, He has power over a crowd.

In this passage, there are demonstrations of the sovereignty of God, in healing the ones He chooses and the ability to walk through a murderous mob. When everything around us appears grim, we can remember that God is ultimately in control. We will be reminded repeatedly of all this as we progress through the Gospel story.

Luke 4:31-44

31 Then He went down to Capernaum, a city of Galilee, and was teaching them on the Sabbaths. **32** And they were astonished at His teaching, for His word was with authority. **33** Now in the synagogue there was a man who had a spirit of an unclean demon. And he cried out with a loud voice, **34** saying, "Let *us* alone! What have we to do with You, Jesus of Nazareth? Did You come to destroy us? I know who You are—the Holy One of God!" **35** But Jesus rebuked him, saying, "Be quiet, and come out of him!" And when the demon had thrown him in *their* midst, it came out of him and did not hurt him. **36** Then they were all amazed and spoke among themselves, saying, "What a word this *is!* For with authority and power He commands the unclean spirits, and they come out." **37** And the report about Him went out into every place in the surrounding region. **38** Now He arose from the synagogue and entered Simon's house. But Simon's wife's mother was sick with a high fever, and they made request of Him concerning her. **39** So He stood over her and rebuked the fever, and it left her. And immediately she arose and served them. **40** When the sun was setting, all those who had any that were sick with various diseases brought them to Him; and He laid His hands on every one of them and healed them. **41** And demons also came out of many, crying out and saying, "You are the Christ, the Son of God!" And He, rebuking *them,* did not allow them to speak, for they knew that He was the Christ. **42** Now when it was day, He departed and went into a deserted place. And the crowd sought Him and came to Him, and tried to keep Him from leaving them; **43** but He said to them, "I must preach the kingdom of God to the other cities also, because for this purpose I have been sent." **44** And He was preaching in the synagogues of Galilee.

Here we see that Jesus' main occupation during His ministry on earth was to teach about God, and expound the meaning of the Scriptures. Christian leaders should remind themselves of this daily. It is easy to be absorbed by necessary administration and neglect the "one thing needful". Generally speaking, there is great ignorance, even amongst Christians, about the contents of the Bible. Leaders do a great service to people by teaching the Gospel. A regular 5-10 minute sermon is insufficient. We all have to spend much time on our work and families. Both are cherished and valued by God. We also need to spend time speaking about Christ.

Jesus confronted Satan in the temptation in the desert. He is now confronted by demonic possession in a member of the congregation. This phenomenon was almost unknown in the Old Testament but Jesus demonstrated His power over it in the Gospels.

People in the West have problems about belief in the devil and demons, but we all see evil around us. The newspapers talk about celebrities who have to "face up to their demons" in the form of drink, addictions, bouts of anger and violence. People have become profoundly disturbed after séances and occult practices. Demon possession is rare and in my professional practice as a surgeon I have seen one possible case which was agreed by a consultant psychiatrist.

From this passage we see a number of features concerning demon possession.

Firstly, we note that the man was controlled by it. He had no power to do anything about the shrieking and yelling that went on in the synagogue that day.

Secondly, the demon was devastated by fear and knew that Jesus had come to destroy the powers of evil and was the Holy One of God. So many of the others present at the gathering had no understanding of Jesus at all. If many in this world do not know who Jesus is, Satan certainly does. James wrote:

You believe that there is one God. You do well. Even the demons believe – and tremble! (James 2: 19)

Thirdly, Jesus demonstrated His power by casting out the demon. Others may try their ceremonies. Travelling exorcists may have used their incantations, but Jesus expelled the demon by His command. This astonished and amazed all those present. We are not told if they believed in Jesus but they could not keep quiet about Him. Luke makes the added clinician's comment and attention to detail that the man was uninjured.

Today, very few may be demon possessed, but many are under the influence of Satan in their blind refusal to believe in Jesus or even enter into meaningful discussion. Paul described Satan as the god of this age or world:

But even if our gospel is veiled, it is veiled to those who are perishing, whose minds the god of this age has blinded, who do not believe, lest the light of the gospel of the glory of Christ, who is in the image of God, should shine on them. (2 Corinthians 4: 3-4)

Christians have no need to fear the devil but we are advised to be aware of him and counter him by putting on the spiritual armour of God. (Ephesians 6: 11-18) "Resist the devil and he will flee from you." (James 4: 7)

After the harrowing and exhausting scenes in the synagogue, Jesus went to Simon Peter's house. Simon's mother-in-law was sick with a fever. Again, Luke makes a physician's extra comment that it was a high fever. The implication is that the poor lady was seriously ill. Jesus had the power to cast out a demon and here, in the private setting of a family home, He heals the patient in front of Him. She recovered so rapidly that she was able to look after Jesus and the accompanying friends. One of the debilitating things about illness is the inability to do anything for anyone. It is such a pleasure to make a cup of tea for a friend or family member after a long period of incapacity.

Later in the day, masses came to the house and He healed them all. No-one need feel excluded from Christ's care. He cares about the needs of each individual. None who come to Him in need and even little faith is turned away.

Finally, we return to Jesus' great occupation to preach the good news of the kingdom of God. He had demonstrated in the wilderness His power to resist temptation and in the synagogue His power over a demon in another person. He went on to teach the kingdom. Instead of the rule of the world, the flesh and the devil in the lives of people He speaks of the lordship of Christ in the lives of those who come to Him. If

Jesus found it important to pray over these great events, so should we be faithful in prayer. "Dear God, please teach us the importance of prayer."

Luke 5:1-11

1 So it was, as the multitude pressed about Him to hear the word of God, that He stood by the Lake of Gennesaret, 2 and saw two boats standing by the lake; but the fishermen had gone from them and were washing *their* nets. 3 Then He got into one of the boats, which was Simon's, and asked him to put out a little from the land. And He sat down and taught the multitudes from the boat. 4 When He had stopped speaking, He said to Simon, "Launch out into the deep and let down your nets for a catch." 5 But Simon answered and said to Him, "Master, we have toiled all night and caught nothing; nevertheless at Your word I will let down the net." 6 And when they had done this, they caught a great number of fish, and their net was breaking. 7 So they signaled to *their* partners in the other boat to come and help them. And they came and filled both the boats, so that they began to sink. 8 When Simon Peter saw *it*, he fell down at Jesus' knees, saying, "Depart from me, for I am a sinful man, O Lord!" 9 For he and all who were with him were astonished at the catch of fish which they had taken; 10 and so also *were* James and John, the sons of Zebedee, who were partners with Simon. And Jesus said to Simon, "Do not be afraid. From now on you will catch men." 11 So when they had brought their boats to land, they forsook all and followed Him.

Here we have a picture of Jesus the popular preacher. The crowds were so dense that the only way He could speak to them was in the posture of a rabbi, seated in a boat. Rabbis carried out much study and quoted Scripture and suggested their opinions and the opinions of others. Unlike the others, Jesus did not need to study. He did not need to balance previous opinions. He was the authority and with sublime sentences, spoke the word of God, because He was and is God.

When it came to preaching, Simon (Peter) was only too ready to listen. However, when it came to fishing he and his friends were the experts. Nevertheless, Peter was willing to let down the net, even though it was the wrong time of day, and probably the wrong place. We learn some lessons from this story of the miraculous catch of fish.

Firstly, we see the divine attribute in Jesus known as omniscience. He knows everything. He knew where the fish were, and He knows everything that is going to happen. Unknown to Peter, He knew that Peter and the others would be evangelists and "catch men". (v.10)

He knows our thinking and our motives and the contents of the deep recesses of our minds. (John 2: 24-25) He knows everything about all people. We often put on a mask to the people around us, and try to give the impression that we are something that we are not. We cannot hide anything from Jesus. We do not know all who truly believe in Him, but Jesus does.

Many months later, Jesus knew that Peter would deny Him. (Luke 22: 54-62) After the resurrection, beside the same Lake, Jesus asked Peter three times, "Do you love Me?' To each question, Peter replied, "You know that I do." On the third time, Peter's reply was even more emphatic, "You know all things." (John 21: 15-19) Jesus' omniscience can be both disturbing and yet comforting.

Secondly, we note that Jesus has a claim to every part of our lives. He is not just for "religious" moments or Sundays alone. He is there for Monday and the rest of the week. He knows all about our work, and all our activities. We can entrust to Him everything we do. Many Christians have said how much the day goes better after committing all to Him.

Peter first referred to Jesus as "Master". (v.5) He then goes on to call Him "Lord". (v.8) He realised Jesus' knowledge or omniscience. He also realised Christ's supreme holiness, and his own sinfulness. (v.8) It is a realisation everyone has to make when they become a Christian.

Thirdly, when confronted with the presence of God, we do not see a light-heartedness that is the characteristic of so many Christian worship meetings, but we see fear. "It is a fearful thing to fall into the hands of the living God." (Hebrews 10: 31)

As we read earlier, in the cases of fear in Zacharias, Mary and the shepherds, Jesus echoed the words, "Do not be afraid." (v.10) We have a tendency to take the kindness of God for granted, or just assume that is something He ought to do. Little do we realise the marvel of His love and concern for us.

Finally, having been with Jesus for some time, these fishermen dropped everything and followed Him. Although we may continue in our education, our work, and families and nothing changes, there is a sense in which we leave our past thinking, preferences, priorities and everything behind.

Therefore, from now on we regard no one according to the flesh... Therefore, if anyone is in Christ, he is a new creation; old things have passed away; behold, all things have become new. (2 Corinthians 5: 16-17)

When we become Christians, we develop new perspectives on so many things. What was trivial in the past now becomes important. What was once important now becomes of secondary importance. One of the main differences between a Christian and others is that the Christian thinks differently.

Luke 5:12-16

12 And it happened when He was in a certain city, that behold, a man who was full of leprosy saw Jesus; and he fell on *his* face and implored Him, saying, "Lord, if You are willing, You can make me clean." **13** Then He put out *His* hand and touched him, saying, "I am willing; be cleansed." Immediately the leprosy left him. **14** And He charged him to tell no one, "But go and show yourself to the priest, and make an offering for your cleansing, as a testimony to them, just as Moses commanded." **15** However, the report went around concerning Him all the more; and great multitudes came together to hear, and to be healed by Him of their infirmities. **16** So He Himself *often* withdrew into the wilderness and prayed.

Leprosy, or Hansen's disease as we know it today, is a chronic infection which attacks the peripheral nerves. It leads to rashes skin, discolouration, loss of pain sense with subsequent long-term damage to the limbs, face and eyes. Ultimately, it destroys the internal organs. It is mildly infectious and is transmitted by sharing living conditions.

There are over five million sufferers in the world today and they are found mainly in tropical countries. Effective drug treatment has only been available for the last few decades. It has to be administered under medical supervision and lasts some months. Whilst drugs in combination heal the infection, they do not alter the deformities and much of the facial and other damage. Skilful and well-timed surgery can improve deformity, cosmetic appearance and some function.

It is thought that in biblical times leprosy included a number of skin conditions. One of the key things about leprosy is that it was regarded as ritually unclean, and the affected person was excluded from society.

In this passage, we learn that the poor man did not demand attention but submitted himself to Jesus' will. (v.12) Luke described the man as full of leprosy. The words "full of" are said to be a term used by medical men of those days. It is clear that the man's whole being had been infected. There was more than hint of desperation about him.

Jesus did a remarkable and scandalous thing. He broke the taboo and removed much of the stigma of disease by means of His touch. On the right and appropriate occasions touch denotes kindness and compassion. It shows a desire to be connected with that person. It tells someone that you care and that things will be all right.

Modern treatments take place over a long time. Jesus healed the man instantaneously and completely and without reference to anything but His command.

The Bible makes a symbolic link between leprosy and human sin. Just as leprosy can affect the whole body, so sin pollutes our minds, our attitudes and our whole being. It is not that in everything we are as bad as we can be; it is that in nothing are we as good as we should be. Sin means me first, and God somewhere else.

Jesus healed the man of his leprosy and He is able to heal us from the penalty, power and pollution of sin. The power of sin is seen all around us, but few of us grasp the significance of its all-pervading nature.

Jesus advised the man to show himself to the priest to confirm the cleansing. Jesus flouted custom by touching the man but showed respect for this instruction from the ceremonial law. Sacrifices were made obsolete by Christ's cross, and so much of the ceremonial law has been superseded, but we should always show a balanced understanding towards it.

Whilst we are told to preach the Gospel to every creature, the healed man was told to inform no one. The reason for this soon became clear when the man could not help but advertise what had happened to him. Jesus became overwhelmed by crowds and had to withdraw to a quiet place. Earlier, in the desert, (ch. 4) Jesus was tempted to become the spectacular celebrity by changing stones

Lev 14.

into bread and by throwing himself off the pinnacle of the Temple. The opportunity for fame and worldly celebrity presented itself at intervals during His ministry. Jesus shunned this status because He wanted people to come to Him as sinners and receive Him in committed faith. The temptation to celebrity has marred the ministry of many aspiring preachers.

Luke 5:17-26

17 Now it happened on a certain day, as He was teaching, that there were Pharisees and teachers of the Law sitting by, who had come out of every town of Galilee, Judea, and Jerusalem. And the power of the Lord was *present* to heal them. **18** Then behold, men brought on a bed a man who was paralyzed, whom they sought to bring in and lay before Him. **19** And when they could not find how they might bring him in, because of the crowd, they went up on the housetop and let him down with *his* bed through the tiling into the midst before Jesus. **20** When He saw their faith, He said to him, "Man, your sins are forgiven you." **21** And the scribes and the Pharisees began to reason, saying, "Who is this who speaks blasphemies? Who can forgive sins but God alone?" **22** But when Jesus perceived their thoughts, He answered and said to them, "Why are you reasoning in your hearts? **23** Which is easier, to say, 'Your sins are forgiven you,' or to say, 'Rise up and walk'? **24** But that you may know that the Son of Man has power on earth to forgive sins"—He said to the man who was paralyzed, "I say to you, arise, take up your bed, and go to your house." **25** Immediately he rose up before them, took up what he had been lying on, and departed to his own house, glorifying God. **26** And they were all amazed, and they glorified God and were filled with fear, saying, "We have seen strange things today!"

In these verses, we are introduced to the Pharisees and teachers of the Law. They would have heard mixed reports about Jesus. Now, many of them wanted to see for themselves. They were part of a six thousand strong meticulous group of law interpreters, and to some extent, law and tradition enforcers. The Pharisees built up a whole system of man-made rules that surrounded the Law to ensure that every possible chance of infringing the Law would be avoided, Instead of fulfilling the Law, it made them even more self-righteous. It became such a burden that instead of uplifting people, the system crushed them. They had their origins in the days of the Exile about six hundred years previously. They believed in the inspiration of the Old Testament Law and prophets, the resurrection, and angels. They also believed in a coming Messiah who would set up a kingdom in Israel, banish oppressors, revive all their interpretations of the Law, and advance temple worship. They were all gathered at the house, there in rows to act as witnesses, counsel, judges and jury. In every subsequent century the attitudes of the Pharisees have had their descendants.

Jesus was teaching and as He spoke, bits started to fall from the roof, as a paralysed man was lowered to His feet.

This passage teaches us more of Jesus' divine nature. Previously, Jesus, with compassion, touched a man, and now He calls another His friend. (Some modern translations use the term "Friend" rather than the more literal "Man"). What a privilege we have that Jesus calls us His friend. We may not even be likeable or attractive or smart. He calls us as a group and, in particular, He addresses us individually. We can continue to wonder that Jesus goes on and on, year after year, not calling us a number or an acquaintance, He calls us His friend. Jesus said:

Greater love has no one than this, than to lay down one's life for his friends. You are My friends if you do whatever I command you. No longer do I call you servants, for a servant does not know what his master is doing, but I have called you friends. (John 15: 13-15)

Then Jesus said to the man that whatever past he had, his sins were forgiven.

That announcement started the muttering and criticism from the Pharisees. They were right to suggest that only God could forgive sins. They truly were right. Little did they realise that the one in front of them really was very God of very God.

Next we notice that Jesus knew what they were thinking. Preachers, who stand in front of congregations can see from people's faces, who are listening, who are enthusiastic, who are resistant, those who wish they were not there. But Luke tells us that Jesus knew exactly what His critics were thinking, right into the recesses of their hearts and minds. Only God can do that.

We do not know the cause of the man's paralysis, but we do know that he was unable to walk. He was, from a human perspective, a likeable man. Although he suffered the misfortune of a devastating paralysis, he did have the good fortune to have four good friends.

Jesus, who we are told had the power to heal, spoke the word and once again we see an instantaneous and complete restoration. The man did not need others to carry his bed or mat, he could handle it himself and walk off. The man who was once dependent on his friends was now independent. At the same time he was dependent on the ministry of Jesus. However independent we might feel, each one of us is totally dependent on Jesus for forgiveness and eternal life.

Luke 5:27-32

27 After these things He went out and saw a tax collector named Levi, sitting at the tax office. And He said to him, "Follow Me." **28** So he left all, rose up, and followed Him. **29** Then Levi gave Him a great feast in his own house. And there were a great number of tax collectors and others who sat down with them. **30** And their scribes and the Pharisees complained against His disciples, saying, "Why do You eat and drink with tax collectors and sinners?" **31** Jesus answered and said to them, "Those who are well have no need of a physician, but those who are sick. **32** I have not come to call *the* righteous, but sinners, to repentance."

Some tax collectors went to hear John the Baptist's trenchant preaching. Levi may have done so, but he also showed interest in Jesus' ministry around Capernaum. Levi, or also known as Matthew, sat at his receipt desk on the main road to Damascus. He extracted a heavy transport tax and also the allowable discretionary, excessive extras. Beside him stood the Roman military authority to enforce his decisions. He was hated by the locals and the religious authorities because of the heavy tax burden and his collaboration with the dreaded Romans. He was a nasty piece of work, not the person you might trust in business, the lowest of the low, the scum of the earth. He was someone righteous people would not associate or eat with. He was not allowed membership or attendance at the synagogue.

When Jesus passed by and called him to follow Him, Matthew made a quick calculation in his mind. Should he continue to earn considerable wealth by hated means, or should he follow the man who healed the sick and spoke wonderful words? Should he change a reliable, steady income for an interesting but uncertain future? His mind was made up. He chose the latter.

When we are called to follow Christ, we know what the present life is but there may be uncertainty about the future. Christ offers meaning, purpose, forgiveness, love, and eternal life with the risk of persecution. Even with the persecution, mental or physical, some would still rather follow Christ. In a way, the option is a "no brainer".

We see here that Jesus was happy to attend social occasions. What shocked and enraged the "righteous Pharisees" was the company He kept. Levi is a name of a priestly tribe, and yet he had sold his soul to the Romans. Jesus was prepared to attend a banquet surrounded by numerous tax collectors. A Pharisee and a law-abiding man would not contaminate themselves with such bad company. Yet, Jesus on this instance and others was made welcome and seemed at ease.

In response to His critics, the reply has resonated down the centuries. Jesus said, "I have not come to call the righteous but sinners to repentance." (v.32) The Pharisees could not imagine that "sinners" also included them.

This is a great challenge to the Christians and the church to welcome everyone to faith in Christ. We should be always there for the "dead-beats and the write-offs". Today, most people believe that they are basically good and decent. It is considered an insult to say otherwise. cf Jer. 🖉9.

Paul's mission to Corinth attracted many of society's rejects, dropouts and uneducated. Jesus' call to repentance means that we can come out of the mess into a life of obedience. Some have difficulty in leaving the mess. As the Apostle, a former Pharisee, remarked in one of his letters:

Do you not know that the unrighteous will not inherit the kingdom of God? Do not be deceived. Neither fornicators, nor idolaters, nor adulterers, nor homosexuals, nor sodomites, nor thieves, nor covetous, nor drunkards, nor revilers, nor extortioners will inherit the kingdom of God. And such were some of you. But you were washed, but you were sanctified, but you were justified in the name of the Lord Jesus and by the Spirit of our God. (1 Corinthians 6: 9-11)

Sadly, there are those who move to a position of judgmental self-righteousness and conform themselves in a small or large way to the attitudes of the Pharisees. Instead, we should have a profound sense of gratitude to God for His complete, unmerited, all-embracing, all-inclusive forgiveness. We should have an attitude of respect with a non-condescending, non-patronizing empathy and appreciation of all we meet.

Jesus' reply to the Pharisees fell on deaf ears. With few exceptions, (John 3: 1-21) they remained unmoved and scandalized.

Luke 5:33-6:5

33 Then they said to Him, "Why do the disciples of John fast often and make prayers, and likewise those of the Pharisees, but Yours eat and drink?" 34 And He said to them, "Can you make the friends of the bridegroom fast while the bridegroom is with them? 35 But the days will come when the bridegroom will be taken away from them; then they will fast in those days." 36 Then He spoke a parable to them: "No one puts a piece from a new garment on an old one; otherwise the new makes a tear, and also the piece that was *taken* out of the new does not match the old. 37 And no one puts new wine into old wineskins; or else the new wine will burst the wineskins and be spilled, and the wineskins will be ruined. 38 But new wine must be put into new wineskins, and both are preserved. 39 And no one, having drunk old *wine,* immediately desires new; for he says, 'The old is better.'" 1 Now it happened on the second Sabbath after the first that He went through the grainfields. And His disciples plucked the heads of grain and ate *them,* rubbing *them* in *their* hands. 2 And some of the Pharisees said to them, "Why are you doing what is not lawful to do on the Sabbath?" 3 But Jesus answering them said, "Have you not even read this, what David did when he was hungry, he and those who were with him: 4 how he went into the house of God, took and ate the showbread, and also gave some to those with him, which is not lawful for any but the priests to eat?" 5 And He said to them, "The Son of Man is also Lord of the Sabbath."

This episode in Jesus' ministry contains a truth that should sink deeply into our souls. Fasting is a discipline that is present in nearly all religions. This and other disciplines are supposed to bring us closer to God. The Pharisees and many other religionists state that we should do all the required practices in order to gain merit or God's favour. If pray, fast, carry out good works and so on, then God will love us more.

Christianity is not like that although we can tend to behave as if it is. First of all, God's love is unconditional. We cannot do anything to gain it. Secondly, it is so vast that He cannot love us any more than He does already.

We do things, like prayer, Bible reading, fellowship, and yes, fasting because He does love us, not in order to make Him love us.

We also see here that Christianity is primarily about relationship. That is, Christ being with us and in us. When Jesus spoke about the bridegroom being with his people, there is a sense of rejoicing; celebration and not fasting. Now in these post-resurrection, post-Pentecost days, Jesus is with us through the Holy Spirit.

Whilst years later the Christians in Antioch (Acts 13:2-3) did fast before the decision to send out missionaries, fasting was not that ascetic, required discipline insisted upon by the Pharisees and their contempories. The example used of wine and wine skins indicated that a new era of change was being brought in by Jesus. This new era was a fulfilment of the Hebrew Scriptures, or the Old Testament as we call it.

An example of a religion dependent on performance and merit is Islam. Islam has its five pillars:

1) The Testimony of faith: "There is no true God but Allah and Muhammad is his prophet".
2) Prayer:
   This is short and performed five times per day.
3) Giving support for the needy.
4) Fasting during the Month of Ramadan.
5) The Pilgrimage to Mecca.

These are the rules that distinguish a Muslim, and the performance of these increases the Muslim's chance of acceptance with God.

In contrast, the mark of Christianity is grace – unmerited favour. The Christian loves God "because He first loved us". (1 John 4: 19)

The next area of criticism surrounded Sabbath observance. Jesus lived as a Jew and obeyed the Torah and made the Sabbath beautiful. Paul states that Jesus was born under the Law:

But when the fullness of the time had come, God sent forth His Son, born of a woman, born under the law...that we might receive the adoption of sons. (Galatians 4: 4-5)

The law allowed people to pluck ears of corn in the field and rub them and eat the grain. (Deuteronomy 23: 25) The religious leaders stated that this was work, equivalent to threshing and reaping. Therefore it was a proscribed activity. In fact, they had developed thousands of rules concerning the Sabbath.

Under Christianity, the Sabbath has given way to the first day of the week, a day when we have the opportunity as Christians to meet together to worship God. May we follow the example of Jesus and seek to worship and glorify God. It is a travesty of true Christianity to be bound and stunted by mere outward observance and deadening formalism.

Not only is Jesus able to forgive sins (5: 24) He is Lord of the Sabbath.

Luke 6:6-16

6 Now it happened on another Sabbath, also, that He entered the synagogue and taught. And a man was there whose right hand was withered. 7 So the scribes and Pharisees watched Him closely, whether He would heal on the Sabbath, that they might find an accusation against Him. 8 But He knew their thoughts, and said to the man who had the withered hand, "Arise and stand here." And he arose and stood. 9 Then Jesus said to them, "I will ask you one thing: Is it lawful on the Sabbath to do good or to do evil, to save life or to destroy?" 10 And when He had looked around at them all, He said to the man, "Stretch out your hand." And he did so, and his hand was restored as whole as the other. 11 But they were filled with rage, and discussed with one another what they might do to Jesus. 12 Now it came to pass in those days that He went out to the mountain to pray, and continued all night in prayer to God. 13 And when it was day, He called His disciples to *Himself*, and from them He chose twelve whom He also named apostles: 14 Simon, whom He also named Peter, and Andrew his brother; James and John; Philip and Bartholomew; 15 Matthew and Thomas; James the *son* of Alphaeus, and Simon called the Zealot; 16 Judas *the son* of James, and Judas Iscariot who also became a traitor.

We note in this passage another confrontation about Sabbath observance. The Pharisees were being secretive in their desire to trap Jesus. They were not concerned about the main issues. They were no longer interested in the content of Jesus' teaching, except when there was a cause about which they could dispute. They had no sense of sympathy for the sick and lame. All they were concerned about was their position and their rules. Whatever the need, it was their legalism that was paramount.

Again, we are unable to make a modern diagnosis of this man's hand condition, but we can say that it was his right hand that was the problem. It would have hampered his daily activities including his ability to earn a reasonable living.

Surgeons and patients are concerned about two things in hand surgery. The first is function. Can the patient do fine tasks? Are they able to have strong different types of grip, and so on? The second is appearance or cosmesis. Does the hand look as normal as possible?

Jesus, in contrast to the secrecy of critics, asked the patient to stand at the front. Jesus did not normally make a show in this way, but He wanted to give His accusers a chance to see the truth for themselves.

He invited the man to stretch out his hand. He was completely healed in both function and appearance.

The anger of the Scribes and Pharisees demonstrated that they had no sense of wonder and delight. All they could think about were their petty issues, and that Jesus healed on the Sabbath.

Many a fellowship has been damaged by arguments over judgmentalism and petty issues. They arise more easily than we would like to think. Prayer and large-heartedness are great qualities for a leadership to have. They are necessary qualities for us all. A person who has a prayerful kind heart is unlikely to gossip.

Today, the system of appointments in business, industry and the professions has become a complicated process. First of all, there have to be the appropriate educational qualifications. Secondly, the candidate has to demonstrate a range of competencies, and thirdly they have to be able to fit into the team. We do not know the criteria Jesus used to choose the apostles but He began with a night of prayer to His Father. He appeared to be looking for the quality of faithful trust. Otherwise they appeared to be the most unpromising group. They had little education. They had no experience in public speaking and communication. With Simon the Zealot, and Matthew the tax collector and collaborator, they were unlikely to form the dream team. There were no priests or teachers of the law, and as far as we know, there was no one with any serious wealth.

Then there was Judas Iscariot. It must have been troubling for Jesus to know that one of the band would, one day, be a traitor.

The presence of Judas reminds us to be aware that not all those in positions of Christian responsibility are truly loyal to Christ.

Even so, these were the men who with later believers would be agents of a process that would go to every part of the world.

They would fail to understand, they would argue, bicker between themselves, but in the end they remained faithful in their mission to take the Gospel to all nations. (Matthew 28: 18-20)

Luke 6:17-45

17 And He came down with them and stood on a level place with a crowd of His disciples and a great multitude of people from all Judea and Jerusalem, and from the seacoast of Tyre and Sidon, who came to hear Him and be healed of their diseases, **18** as well as those who were tormented with unclean spirits. And they were healed. **19** And the whole multitude sought to touch Him, for power went out from Him and healed *them* all. **20** Then He lifted up His eyes toward His disciples, and said: "Blessed *are you* poor, For yours is the kingdom of God. **21** Blessed *are you* who hunger now, For you shall be filled. Blessed *are you* who weep now, For you shall laugh. **22** Blessed are you when men hate you, And when they exclude you, And revile *you,* and cast out your name as evil, For the Son of Man's sake. **23** Rejoice in that day and leap for joy! For indeed your reward *is* great in heaven, For in like manner their fathers did to the prophets. **24** But woe to you who are rich, For you have received your consolation. **25** Woe to you who are full, For you shall hunger. Woe to you who laugh now, For you shall mourn and weep. **26** Woe to you when all men speak well of you, For so did their fathers to the false prophets. **27** But I say to you who hear: Love your enemies, do good to those who hate you, **28** bless those who curse you, and pray for those who spitefully use you. **29** To him who strikes you on the *one* cheek, offer the other also. And from him who takes away your cloak, do not withhold *your* tunic either. **30** Give to everyone who asks of you. And from him who takes away your goods do not ask *them* back. **31** And just as you want men to do to you, you also do to them likewise. **32** But if you love those who love you, what credit is that to you? For even sinners love those who love them. **33** And if you do good to those who do good to you, what credit is that to you? For even sinners do the same. **34** And if you lend *to those* from whom you hope to receive back, what credit is that to you? For even sinners lend to sinners to receive as much back. **35** But love your enemies, do good, and lend, hoping for nothing in return; and your reward will be great, and you will be sons of the Most High. For He is kind to the unthankful and evil. **36** Therefore be merciful, just as your Father also is merciful. **37** Judge not, and you shall not be judged. Condemn not, and you shall not be condemned. Forgive, and you will be forgiven. **38** Give, and it will be given to you: good measure, pressed down, shaken together, and running over will be put into your bosom. For with the same measure that you use, it will be measured back to you." **39** And He spoke a parable to them: "Can the blind lead the blind? Will they not both fall into the ditch? **40** A disciple is not above his teacher, but everyone who is perfectly trained will be like his teacher. **41** And why do you look at the speck in your brother's eye, but do not perceive the plank in your own eye? **42** Or how can you say to your brother, 'Brother, let me remove the speck that *is* in your eye,' when you yourself do not see the plank that *is* in your own eye? Hypocrite! First remove the plank from your own eye, and then you will see clearly to remove the speck that is in your brother's eye. **43** For a good tree does not bear bad fruit, nor does a bad tree bear good fruit. **44** For every tree is known by its own fruit. For *men* do not gather figs from thorns, nor do they gather grapes from a bramble bush. **45** A good man out of the good treasure of his heart brings forth good; and an evil man out of the evil treasure of his heart brings forth evil. For out of the abundance of the heart his mouth speaks."

We now consider this 1 minute or so sermon which we find in Luke. There is a larger version of a similar sermon related in Matthew, and no doubt, they were wise summaries of longer discourses. In Luke it is, "The Sermon on the Plain". In Matthew it is, "The Sermon on the Mount."

I remember as a small boy reading the early part of this and I thought that there were some people who were poor and others who wept, and still others who found themselves hated and so on. To these different and diverse groups, Jesus pronounced the unlikely benefit of being blessed. I was really struck by that. Now there was and still is a lot of truth in this interpretation.

However, later I was informed that all these attributes, or beatitudes as we call them, were all part of a description of one and the same person, namely the Christian. This is the description of what each and every Christian is or should be.

Every Christian should be poor; that is, know their need of God. Every Christian, at some stage, mourns their sins and is repentant. Every Christian should hunger after a greater relationship with God. In fact, it can be regarded as an acid test of Christian commitment. Every Christian should weep about the state of the world. Finally the Christian can expect hatred and persecution. Years later, Peter made this startling comment about persecution:

Beloved, do not think it strange concerning the fiery trial which is to try you, as though some strange thing happened to you; but rejoice to the extent that you partake of Christ's sufferings, that when His glory is revealed, you may also be glad with exceeding joy. If you are reproached for the name of Christ, blessed are you, for the Spirit of glory and of God rests upon you. On their part He is blasphemed, but on your part He is glorified.(1Peter 4:12-14)

The extraordinary thing is that all these particular experiences are blessed. These are among the unworldly and unfathomable paradoxes of Christianity.

Then Luke records Jesus as making some striking remarks which are the opposite of the things we strive to do and spend much time seeking to achieve. We seek to be well off, well fed. We chase laughter and popularity. Jesus reminded us that these things are temporary and are built on a poor foundation.

Then comes another surprise. The Messiah was supposed to banish Israel's enemies. Yet here He said – love your enemies, and pray for them.

 Later He added to the prevailing golden rule. Other religions and philosophies taught that we should not do to others those things we would not like to be done to us. Jesus turned a negative into a positive. "And just as you want men to do to you, you also do to them." (v.31)

I am always very moved when Christian relatives of murder victims are interviewed by the media. They almost invariably express concern and prayer for the murderer. I find no other people who do that.

I remember giving a lesson on the King James Version of the Bible to students in a teacher-training college in North East China. Although the Chinese authorities shunned all types of religion, they did regard the King James Version as an example of English literature. I shared these sayings of Jesus with the students, and one asked the most relevant of questions, "How do I love my enemy?"

I do not remember my reply but the frank truth is that no-one can keep all the sayings of this sermon. In fact, that is one of the main points. Only Jesus lived up to what He taught. Here is Peter's further comment from his first epistle:

For to this you were called, because Christ also suffered for us, leaving us an example, that you should follow His steps: "Who committed no sin, nor was deceit found in His mouth"; who, when He was reviled, did not revile in return; when He suffered, He did not threaten, but committed Himself to Him who judges righteously; who Himself bore our sins in His own body on the tree, that we, having died to sins, might live for righteousness—by whose stripes you were healed. For you were like sheep going astray, but have now returned to the Shepherd and Overseer of your souls. (1 Peter 2: 21-25)

Peter invites us to the foot of the cross in repentance and faith. Only in that way will we be able to approach the tenets of Jesus' great sermon. It is a sermon that has challenged, intrigued and mystified millions down the centuries. No-one has ever gone as far as Jesus in these sayings. They are the absolute perfection of love. Many ridicule them as impractical and unworkable. In that, they may not realize how right they are. Sadly, most critics do not even aspire to its teaching.

Luke 6:46-49

46 "But why do you call Me 'Lord, Lord,' and not do the things which I say? **47** Whoever comes to Me, and hears My sayings and does them, I will show you whom he is like: **48** He is like a man building a house, who dug deep and laid the foundation on the rock. And when the flood arose, the stream beat vehemently against that house, and could not shake it, for it was founded on the rock. **49** But he who heard and did nothing is like a man who built a house on the earth without a foundation, against which the stream beat vehemently; and immediately it fell. And the ruin of that house was great."

There are some who even go as far as calling Jesus, "Lord, Lord", but they let these words go over them as if they had made no impression at all. Some give Christianity lip-service. Examples are the reading of prayers at a civic service or a perfunctory recital of liturgy by a faithless minister. There may even be a quest for respectability. Such people are becoming fewer in number, as the rise of secular thought makes it no longer respectable to give even a superficial acceptance of Christianity.

However, in all cultures we realize that to build a house that will stand, we need to build a house that has a firm foundation. Unless the house is being built on stilts over a lake, then the best secure foundation is rock. As a young boy I lived near a mining area. As we drove through, one could see large cracks on the walls of houses. Sometimes efforts were made to shore up the walls by the use of wooden buttresses. The problem was that the underground mining was too near the surface and the foundations were insufficient to prevent serious subsidence and damage.

From this passage we learn that the Christian life needs a good foundation. This should always be clear in the process of evangelism.

Firstly, that foundation does not depend on going through the motions of church attendance and other kinds of religiosity. Moreover, it should not depend on God granting favours to make me successful, wealthy or even popular. We come to Christ because we want to say "Yes!" to the teachings of Jesus which have just been spoken. It means that we come in repentance to the foot of the cross to find forgiveness and salvation. It means that we want to "put on the Lord Jesus Christ". It means that we intend to do business with God on His terms. The Apostle Paul was very aware of what it meant to have Jesus as our foundation:

According to the grace of God, which was given to me, as a wise master builder I have laid the foundation, and another builds on it. But let each one take heed how he builds on it. For no other foundation can anyone lay than that which is laid, which is Jesus Christ. Now if anyone builds on this foundation with gold, silver, precious stones, wood, hay, straw, each one's work will become clear; for the Day will declare it, because it will be revealed by fire; and the fire will test each one's work, of what sort it is. If anyone's work which he has built on it endures, he will receive a reward. If anyone's work is burned, he will suffer loss; but he himself will be saved, yet so as through fire. (1 Corinthians 3: 10-15)

Secondly, we note that in life there will be great storms. With climate change, many areas of the world have suffered severe flooding, with loss of life and severe damage to property. There will also be personal storms. These include unfulfilled expectation, failed relationships, financial difficulty, and loss of health. Will we hold fast to Christ in all of this? Will we still look to the heavenward goal?

Thirdly, I have known people whose faith was wrecked because they did not have a right beginning, they did not have a good foundation. If we think our foundation is shaky, we need to start digging again. We must not stop until we know that we are secure. Let us mark Jesus' warning that those who do not heed His words will collapse and suffer a complete destruction. (v.49)

Luke 7:1-10

1 Now when He concluded all His sayings in the hearing of the people, He entered Capernaum. **2** And a certain centurion's servant, who was dear to him, was sick and ready to die. **3** So when he heard about Jesus, he sent elders of the Jews to Him, pleading with Him to come and heal his servant. **4** And when they came to Jesus, they begged Him earnestly, saying that the one for whom He should do this was deserving, **5** "for he loves our nation, and has built us a synagogue." **6** Then Jesus went with them. And when He was already not far from the house, the centurion sent friends to Him, saying to Him, "Lord, do not trouble Yourself, for I am not worthy that You should enter under my roof. **7** Therefore I did not even think myself worthy to come to You. But say the word, and my servant will be healed. **8** For I also am a man placed under authority, having soldiers under me. And I say to one, 'Go,' and he goes; and to another, 'Come,' and he comes; and to my servant, 'Do this,' and he does *it*." **9** When Jesus heard these things, He marveled at him, and turned around and said to the crowd that followed Him, "I say to you, I have not found such great faith, not even in Israel!" **10** And those who were sent, returning to the house, found the servant well who had been sick.

In this passage we have a description of Jesus' encounter with a Roman soldier, a centurion. On reading the New Testament, we find that Jesus, far from being embittered and hostile towards soldiers, was very kind to them. They seem to have received what we would now describe as "a good press".

Comparisons with our own times are difficult, but I think we could say that the nearest modern day equivalent to a centurion is a major. However, these were men who came up from the ranks. They knew what it was like to be in battle. They knew what it was like to see violence and brutality. They knew what it was like to kill someone. They knew how to repress a people.

This man was part of an army of occupation. Something and

someone the Jewish people resented bitterly. From time to time, there were uprisings, which were ruthlessly crushed. When a centurion gave orders, things happened, according to instructions, with no excuses, and no messing. He too was under authority, and received orders, which had to be carried out to the letter.

Although at that time, Jewish people often expressed their distaste for the Gentile or non-Jew, there were some from the surrounding nations who felt dissatisfaction with many aspects of the prevailing culture and attitudes. They felt attracted to the Jewish idea of there being one creator God, who displayed a character of justice, fairness, and moral consistency. They were allowed to sit at the back of the synagogue and listen in to the reading, prayers and teaching. If they wished to obey the observances of the law they could join up and were then called proselytes.

Whilst not a proselyte, this man had a significant love and admiration for Israel, and had gone so far as to build a synagogue.

We do not know the centurion's name but we do know that he had a loyal servant who was a good man, did a good job, was reliable, and may have even become a friend. However, in those days, life was far more precarious than it is now. The servant had fallen sick and was dying. Life expectancy was less than half that of modern Europe. No doubt, the centurion had heard of Jesus' spreading fame, His healings, teachings and actions. The soldier decided to do something about his servant's illness. He requested a delegation of Jews to go and ask Jesus to come and heal his servant.

The Jews, unlike the humble centurion, informed Jesus that it was something He ought to do.

As Jesus approached the house, an even more remarkable request came. The centurion knew all about the receiving and giving orders. He knew that Jews would become ceremonially unclean if they entered his house, so he, a symbol of Roman rule, said that he did not deserve to have Jesus come under his roof. "Say the word, and my servant shall be healed." (v.7) Jesus replied that He had not seen faith like this in the whole of Israel. It was a stunning observation and rebuke to the others around Him. They had all the privileges of being the receivers of the Law and the prophets, but it was this foreign soldier who had been commended. The servant was made completely well.

Soldiers are part of a system of a fallen and fractured world. They are there frequently to maintain or impose peace. Sometimes they do just that as in the case of this Roman centurion. At other times they are called upon to witness and do terrible things, as we are all too aware from the history of warfare. In fact, Jesus was amazed that the greatest faith that He found in the whole of Israel was that of a Gentile Roman soldier. Faith in Jesus can come from the most unlikely quarter!

Luke 7:11-17

11 Now it happened, the day after, *that* He went into a city called Nain; and many of His disciples went with Him, and a large crowd. **12** And when He came near the gate of the city, behold, a dead man was being carried out, the only son of his mother; and she was a widow. And a large crowd from the city was with her. **13** When the Lord saw her, He had compassion on her and said to her, "Do not weep." **14** Then He came and touched the open coffin, and those who carried *him* stood still. And He said, "Young man, I say to you, arise." **15** So he who was dead sat up and began to speak. And He presented him to his mother. **16** Then fear came upon all, and they glorified God, saying, "A great prophet has risen up among us"; and, "God has visited His people." **17** And this report about Him went throughout all Judea and all the surrounding region.

There is nothing more heart-wrenching or grievous for a parent than to lose a son. The Bible describes death as the last enemy. We all know that one day we will die, but it is even more difficult to outlive our children. I remember seeing a ninety-five year old lady who came to our outpatient clinic. She had outlived her husband and all her five children.

The only son of this poor widow was probably the main breadwinner. This would have compounded her grief, filled her with a sense of hopelessness, being without any means. The accompanying mourners would have been weeping out of custom and duty. Her weeping was out of intense grief.

Once again, we see this profoundly moving note of compassion in our Lord. There are a billion stars in our galaxy, and over a billion galaxies in our universe. Yet at the origin and centre of all this, there is a heart of love and kindness. The Psalmist was transfixed by the wonder of it all:

When I consider Your heavens, the work of Your fingers, the moon and the stars, which You have ordained; What is man, that You are mindful of him? and the son of man, that You visit him? For You have made him a little lower than the angels, and You have crowned him with glory and honor. You made him to have dominion over the works of Your hands; You have put all things under his feet: (Psalm 8:3-6)

Jesus urged her not to weep. Our words of comfort are real in words, but at best only limited in action. Jesus was able to say to the corpse, "Get up," and that is exactly what happened. Jesus responded to the lady's grief. We are not told as to whether she had faith or had even heard of Jesus. He responded to her need.

Jesus had shown His power over temptation and over demons. He had divine knowledge about the location of fish and the deep recesses of the human heart. He was Lord of the Sabbath and able to keep company with anyone in society. He touched lepers and healed the sick by the touch of His hand or the command of His voice. There appeared to be no ritual or incantation, which was a feature of His many false contempories. His speech had no rivals. He now shows in His gentle and compassionate way His power, even over death.

One day in the future, that young man died. One day, we shall die, but Jesus through His resurrection has conquered death. One day we, Christians, shall reign with Him:

For as in Adam all die, even so in Christ shall all be made alive. But each one in his own order: Christ the firstfruits, afterward those who are Christ's at His coming. Then comes the end, when He delivers the kingdom to God the Father, when He puts an end to all rule and all authority and power. For He must reign till He has put all enemies under His feet. The last enemy that will be destroyed is death. For "He has put all things under His feet." (1 Corinthians 15: 22-27)

The world has its methods in trying to smooth over the news of death. They may have an emollient resignation. They may give their fulsome obituaries, but really they offer nothing. Only the Christian has the hope of everlasting life. Only the Christian can have a true perspective on life, death and eternity.

The widowed mother had her son restored to her, but in Jesus the

Messiah, she also had the hope of everlasting life.

The crowd were filled with awe and acknowledged Jesus as a prophet. Perhaps later, some of them came to know Jesus as their "Lord and God".

Luke 7:18-35

18 Then the disciples of John reported to him concerning all these things. **19** And John, calling two of his disciples to *him*, sent *them* to Jesus, saying, "Are You the Coming One, or do we look for another?" **20** When the men had come to Him, they said, "John the Baptist has sent us to You, saying, 'Are You the Coming One, or do we look for another?'" **21** And that very hour He cured many of infirmities, afflictions, and evil spirits; and to many blind He gave sight. **22** Jesus answered and said to them, "Go and tell John the things you have seen and heard: that *the* blind see, *the* lame walk, *the* lepers are cleansed, *the* deaf hear, *the* dead are raised, *the* poor have the gospel preached to them. **23** And blessed is *he* who is not offended because of Me." **24** When the messengers of John had departed, He began to speak to the multitudes concerning John: "What did you go out into the wilderness to see? A reed shaken by the wind? **25** But what did you go out to see? A man clothed in soft garments? Indeed those who are gorgeously appareled and live in luxury are in kings' courts. **26** But what did you go out to see? A prophet? Yes, I say to you, and more than a prophet. **27** This is *he* of whom it is written: 'Behold, I send My messenger before Your face, Who will prepare Your way before You.' **28** For I say to you, among those born of women there is not a greater prophet than John the Baptist; but he who is least in the kingdom of God is greater than he." **29** And when all the people heard *Him*, even the tax collectors justified God, having been baptized with the baptism of John. **30** But the Pharisees and lawyers rejected the will of God for themselves, not having been baptized by him. **31** And the Lord said, "To what then shall I liken the men of this generation, and what are they like? **32** They are like children sitting in the marketplace and calling to one another, saying: 'We played the flute for you, And you did not dance; We mourned to you, And you did not weep.' **33** For John the Baptist came neither eating bread nor drinking wine, and you say, 'He has a demon.' **34** The Son of Man has come eating and drinking, and you say, 'Look, a glutton and a winebibber, a friend of tax collectors and sinners!' **35** But wisdom is justified by all her children."

John the Baptist had been faithful in his task as a forerunner of the Messiah. He had preached repentance to thousands. He employed the rite of baptism as a symbol of the washing away of sins. People came to him from Jerusalem and all the surrounding country. He was at the centre of a national renewal. He spoke of a coming Messiah.

John languished in jail because of his criticism of Herod's marital unfaithfulness. All that was in front of him was a long imprisonment or early violent death.

Commentators have disagreed as to the motive of his question, "Are You the Coming One, or do we look for another?" (v.19)

In the loneliness and poor conditions of a cell, was his faith wavering? Was he trying to force Jesus' hand? Alternatively, was he trying to move the allegiance of his disciples from himself to Jesus? Most commentators appear to support the latter notion.

Either way, Jesus did not conform to the then current view as to how the Messiah would present. The intellectuals of Jesus' day would have thought that Jesus should have established Himself as a key political figure in Jerusalem and gained popularity amongst the teachers of the Law and other religious figures. Members of Jesus' wider family certainly thought that. (John 7: 3-5) They expected high position, respectable clothes and removal of the Romans. Instead we see a man with few means, worker's clothes and uneducated followers, teaching in the less fashionable areas of Galilee.

As a proof of Messiahship, Jesus heals, opens, cleanses, raises and preaches good news to the poor. To this day, Jewish rabbis discount Jesus as Messiah for many of the reasons given when Jesus was on this earth. Are we prepared to accept what was not expected? Are we prepared to believe the purposes of God and those faithful Gospel writers?

The modern skeptic impugns the veracity and honesty of those writers. In other words, the whole story was part of a conspiracy. Conspiracies do not survive under pressure and penetrating scrutiny. Few have had to undergo the cross-examination and persecution of those apostles and early believers. They held to their beliefs. Not one of the apostles wavered over their testimony.

Jesus spoke plainly when He said, "Blessed is he who is not offended because (or, who does not fall away on account) of Me." (v.23)

Jesus' tribute to John the Baptist was lavish in its praise. "There is none greater than John." Jesus makes the surprising statement, "Yet he who is least in the kingdom of God is greater than he."

How is this? The reason is not because of quality or ability but because of grace, a new privilege, God's gifts and the new Gospel era. Before Jesus, the Holy Spirit was given to the few. Afterwards the Holy Spirit was given to all who truly believe. Paul put it in this way:

But the Scripture has confined all under sin, that the promise by faith in Jesus Christ might be given to those who believe. But before faith came, we were kept under guard by the law, kept for the faith which would afterward be revealed. Therefore the law was our tutor to bring us to Christ, that we might be justified by faith. But after faith has come, we are no longer under a tutor. (Galatians 3: 22-25)

The last few verses of this passage remind us that Jesus and the Gospel are suitable to every kind of person, the introvert and the extrovert, those who like to socialize and those who are more solitary and contemplative. This has been demonstrated in the make-up of the apostles and the subsequent church of God.

Visit any church with a congregation of over fifteen and this will be shown to be true. We are in many ways different in personality and ability, yet together make up a functioning body. The point Jesus made is that whatever approach, and whatever evidence, there will always be those who do not and will not believe.

"We played the flute for you,
And you did not dance;
We mourned to you,
And you did not weep." (v.32)

Skeptics always seem to want one more sign, one more piece of intellectual proof.

To quote from an account given by Jesus later in this Gospel:

"But if one goes to them from the dead, they will repent " But he said to him, "If they do not hear Moses and the prophets, neither will they be persuaded though one rise from the dead." (Luke 16: 30-31)

In spite of all that John the Baptist and Jesus did, said and looked like, there would always be those, who for their own reasons, would be insistent in their unbelief. "There are none so blind as those who won't see."

Luke 7:36-50

36 Then one of the Pharisees asked Him to eat with him. And He went to the Pharisee's house, and sat down to eat. **37** And behold, a woman in the city who was a sinner, when she knew that *Jesus* sat at the table in the Pharisee's house, brought an alabaster flask of fragrant oil, **38** and stood at His feet behind *Him* weeping; and she began to wash His feet with her tears, and wiped *them* with the hair of her head; and she kissed His feet and anointed *them* with the fragrant oil. **39** Now when the Pharisee who had invited Him saw *this,* he spoke to himself, saying, "This Man, if He were a prophet, would know who and what manner of woman *this is* who is touching Him, for she is a sinner." **40** And Jesus answered and said to him, "Simon, I have something to say to you." So he said, "Teacher, say it." **41** "There was a certain creditor who had two debtors. One owed five hundred denarii, and the other fifty. **42** And when they had nothing with which to repay, he freely forgave them both. Tell Me, therefore, which of them will love him more?" **43** Simon answered and said, "I suppose the *one* whom he forgave more." And He said to him, "You have rightly judged." **44** Then He turned to the woman and said to Simon, "Do you see this woman? I entered your house; you gave Me no water for My feet, but she has washed My feet with her tears and wiped *them* with the hair of her head. **45** You gave Me no kiss, but this woman has not ceased to kiss My feet since the time I came in. **46** You did not anoint My head with oil, but this woman has anointed My feet with fragrant oil. **47** Therefore I say to you, her sins, which *are* many, are forgiven, for she loved much. But to whom little is forgiven, *the same* loves little." **48** Then He said to her, "Your sins are forgiven." **49** And those who sat at the table with Him began to say to themselves, "Who is this who even forgives sins?" **50** Then He said to the woman, "Your faith has saved you. Go in peace."

In those days and that part of the world, dinners attended by dignitaries were seldom private occasions. The guests would recline around the low table and then eat and talk about the issues of the day. The town's people would gather round in corners of the room, or congregate outside open windows and listen. The modern equivalent would be listening to a radio or TV panel.

From these evenings they would learn about the news, and gossip. Afterwards, they might be able to eat some of the leftover food.

This dinner was accompanied by a scandalous incident. A woman arrived unexpectedly. The Bible described her as a sinner or sinful woman. (v. 37) It was clear that she was a prostitute. Whilst we are all responsible for our actions, Jesus seemed to have more insight into her situation than His contemporaries.

In the last few decades, with the practice of human trafficking and exploitation, it is clear that the situation is more complex than might be understood on superficial examination. More often than not, criminal gangs exploit women for their own profit. The title, "the oldest profession", hides a history of control, violence and prolonged cruelty, sometimes to the death of the woman. Women in these situations are mainly sinned against. Only in recent years have lawmakers in some Northern countries tried to deal with the demand side of the "sex industry".

The arrival of this woman, her anointing with the most expensive perfume, and weeping over Jesus' feet was considered outrageous. Her hair should have been covered rather than let down and used to wipe Jesus' feet. There is something about the presence of Jesus that makes the genuine enquirer convicted by guilt. It makes no difference as whether the seeker is respectable or disreputable, the Holy Spirit works in the heart to convict of sin. (John 16: 8) God was at work in her heart.

It appears that the Pharisee invited Jesus to his house in order to find fault rather than because of any kind of respect or recognition. He made no attempt to make Jesus particularly welcome with the usual greeting of anointing and foot washing. Simon the Pharisee was respectable, and believed that he obeyed every tenet of the Law. He held the erroneous notion that he was right with God, by virtue of both his birth and performance, and considered that this woman was totally beyond redemption. He was insensitive in his observance of the quality of Jesus' life and any prompting of his conscience by the Holy Spirit. He was blind to his own self-centred sin.

The woman wanted a new beginning. She was forgiven much and

was enabled to lead a new life. We see from Jesus' parting words that forgiveness by God and a life of renewal begins a life of peace and assured hope. (v.50)

Luke tells us much about Jesus' kind treatment of a number of different groups. Women are amongst the foremost in His affirmation.

One final point to remember is that one of Jesus' ancestors mentioned in His genealogy is Rahab. (Matthew 1: 5) She was a Gentile prostitute who was converted to God and given a new life with the people of God. Some believe she married one of the two Israelites who went to spy out the city of Jericho before its capture. (Joshua 2: 1-21) There is no-one too disreputable as to be outside God's reach and kingdom.

Luke 8:1-15

1 Now it came to pass, afterward, that He went through every city and village, preaching and bringing the glad tidings of the kingdom of God. And the twelve *were* with Him, **2** and certain women who had been healed of evil spirits and infirmities—Mary called Magdalene, out of whom had come seven demons, **3** and Joanna the wife of Chuza, Herod's steward, and Susanna, and many others who provided for Him from their substance. **4** And when a great multitude had gathered, and they had come to Him from every city, He spoke by a parable: **5** "A sower went out to sow his seed. And as he sowed, some fell by the wayside; and it was trampled down, and the birds of the air devoured it. **6** Some fell on rock; and as soon as it sprang up, it withered away because it lacked moisture. **7** And some fell among thorns, and the thorns sprang up with it and choked it. **8** But others fell on good ground, sprang up, and yielded a crop a hundredfold." When He had said these things He cried, "He who has ears to hear, let him hear!" **9** Then His disciples asked Him, saying, "What does this parable mean?" **10** And He said, "To you it has been given to know the mysteries of the kingdom of God, but to the rest *it is given* in parables, that 'Seeing they may not see, And hearing they may not understand.' **11** Now the parable is this: The seed is the word of God. **12** Those by the wayside are the ones who hear; then the devil comes and takes away the word out of their hearts, lest they should believe and be saved. **13** But the ones on the rock *are those* who, when they hear, receive the word with joy; and these have no root, who believe for a while and in time of temptation fall away. **14** Now the ones *that* fell among thorns are those who, when they have heard, go out and are choked with cares, riches, and pleasures of life, and bring no fruit to maturity. **15** But the ones *that* fell on the good ground are those who, having heard the word with a noble and good heart, keep *it* and bear fruit with patience."

The first three verses remind us of the high place Jesus has given to the status of women. Mary, Elizabeth, and Anna played prominent roles at the beginning of Luke's gospel. Women gave support during Jesus' ministry. Jesus loved to visit the home of Martha and Mary. Women were Jesus' only friends at the foot of the cross, except for John, and later on, one of the thieves and later still, the Roman centurion. All the other disciples had fled. Women were first to visit the tomb on that Easter morning. Mary Magdelene was the first to see the risen Lord Jesus. Women were present in the room on that first day of the church, at Pentecost.

Women have been main providers of social services. They have been and are distinguished hymn writers. They have been powerhouses of prayer all through the history of the church. Their work has not always been given proper appreciation. Let us remember Jesus appreciated and gave proper recognition to their enormous contribution.

The parable of the sower has been already explained by Jesus Himself. It would be foolish to try and add to His interpretation.

Nevertheless, it is worth making a few side points. From this parable we can note that just as it is hard work to be a successful farmer, there is also hard work and labour involved in the proclamation of the gospel. Even in times of revival, the workers have grown weary. Jesus Himself was tired after a day's hard work. Gospel ministry is no easy fix, it has no short cuts and is no occupation for the idle.

Secondly, those involved in ministry, that is all of us, will encounter disappointment. There are those whom we thought would respond to the Gospel who have failed to do so. There are those who appeared to make a good start but have fallen away. It is something that can disappoint and yet it is also something that we should expect. In spite of apparent reverses, we should not lose heart.

Thirdly, we note that falling away in this parable is not due to the power of human reason, depth of learning or any kind of superior intellect, but that old trio, the world, the flesh and the devil.

The seed that fell on the path had the word taken away by the devil. Those that fell on the rock fell away due to the testing of the world. The seed that fell amongst thorns were choked away by the enticements of the flesh. There have been many young promising doctors and others who have fallen away from the faith at the beginning of their career and on leaving the fellowship they once enjoyed at college.

Finally, let us remember that in spite of all the heartaches and disappointments there are those who receive and carry on in their most precious faith. We see from its earliest and unpromising beginnings and persecutions, the church has spread all around the globe. This is due to the seeds that multiplied, some even to one hundred times.

Luke 8:16-21

16 "No one, when he has lit a lamp, covers it with a vessel or puts *it* under a bed, but sets *it* on a lampstand, that those who enter may see the light. **17** For nothing is secret that will not be revealed, nor *anything* hidden that will not be known and come to light. **18** Therefore take heed how you hear. For whoever has, to him *more* will be given; and whoever does not have, even what he seems to have will be taken from him." **19** Then His mother and brothers came to Him, and could not approach Him because of the crowd. **20** And it was told Him *by some,* who said, "Your mother and Your brothers are standing outside, desiring to see You." **21** But He answered and said to them, "My mother and My brothers are these who hear the word of God and do it."

The parable of the lamp is an extension to the parable of the sower. The Christian has two types of option. They can try to live life as if the Gospel has never made a difference. They look the same as before. They are replicas of those around them and they go with the flow.

On the other hand, if the Gospel has taken root and Jesus is the Lord of your life, then people will notice. They will notice the change of language and lack of swearing. They will notice a sympathetic demeanour. They will see stances for what is right. They will receive messages of encouragement to believe. We do not always get it right, but our Lord described us as like a light which can be seen by all around.

God can add to the person who stands for Him. If we seek His will and endeavour to enlarge our Christian experience and the presence of God, then God produces the growth.

We also have the solemn warning that God knows everything. He knows the secrets of the heart. (Psalm 44:21) If we give a token and superficial allegiance, with lack of spiritual ambition, then even this minute token will be taken away.

Jesus' relationship with His family is a fascinating sub-plot going through the New Testament. Initially, they did not think that Jesus measured up to their idea as to what a Messiah should do. They were concerned that Jesus suffered from what we might call stress. They were influenced by their religious leaders who thought that the Messiah would:

1) Be accepted by the religious leaders.

2) Establish renewal of reforms of Temple worship.

3) Announce a rigorous observance of the Law, according to their traditions.

4) Demonstrate to everyone the political dominance of Israel and impose a geographical peace.

5) Get rid of enemies, in particular, the Romans.

6) Provide a source of food.

Instead Jesus preached good news to the poor, proclaimed freedom to captives, recovery of sight to the blind, and release for the oppressed, and did so many other things that we have already seen.

John tells us that they "did not believe in Him." (John 7: 5) However, at some point between the cross and ascension they did come to believe. Two of them, James and Jude, wrote letters which became part of our New Testament.

Do you have relatives who do not believe? Do not stop praying for them. I tell this story of a ninety something year old lady who prayed for her son for seventy years. He came to the Lord at seventy years of age.

Some relatives spend their lives in unbelief and go to their graves, totally unresponsive to the Gospel and unsaved. Others come to Christ even on their deathbeds, because of the grace of God and the examples and prayers of their relatives. Do continue to pray. I know many have prayed for years for loved ones. Don't stop!

The final verse of this passage has an extraordinary statement which we can barely take in if we really care to take note.

Jesus is the Son of God, the Saviour of the world, Lord of life, very God of very God, who dwells in unapproachable light, and is the light of the world and through whom and for whom the world was made, the exact representation of God.

He says this about you. "My mother and brothers are these who hear the word of God and do it." (v.21) This is not a fractious relationship full of tensions, as can be so often experienced in our own families. This is our relationship with the Son of God. He invites us to be members of His family.

Luke 8:22-25

Hopeless Situations

22 Now it happened, on a certain day, that He got into a boat with His disciples. And He said to them, "Let us cross over to the other side of the lake." And they launched out. **23** But as they sailed He fell asleep. And a windstorm came down on the lake, and they were filling *with water,* and were in jeopardy. **24** And they came to Him and awoke Him, saying, "Master, Master, we are perishing!" Then He arose and rebuked the wind and the raging of the water. And they ceased, and there was a calm. **25** But He said to them, "Where is your faith?" And they were afraid, and marveled, saying to one another, "Who can this be? For He commands even the winds and water, and they obey Him!"

The journey across the Lake Galilee and the calming of the storm is recounted in three of the gospels. It is important for a number of reasons.

Firstly, we have both a picture of Christ's humanity and also His divinity. His humanity was demonstrated by His obvious fatigue and need of sleep. This was part of the humbling and self-emptying that took place when Jesus became a man:

Let this mind be in you which was also in Christ Jesus, who, being in the form of God, did not consider it robbery to be equal with God, but made Himself of no reputation, taking the form of a bondservant, and coming in the likeness of men. And being found in appearance as a man, He humbled Himself and became obedient to the point of death, even the death of the cross. (Philippians 2:5-8)

Modern science is able to do much to make our lives comfortable and protect us from the ravages of hostile weather. We are able to predict the weather, but no-one can control it. To the amazement of His disciples and to all of us – Jesus was able to command the storm to cease. Only God can do that. The early centuries of the church were dominated by arguments about Jesus' nature. Was He all God or all man? Was He part God and part man, or any combination of these suggestions? This passage in Luke supports the ultimate and true verdict that Jesus was and is both fully God and fully man at all times. At some moments we see more of His manhood and at others, we see more of His Godhead:

Therefore God also has highly exalted Him and given Him the name which is above every name, that at the name of Jesus every knee should bow, of those in heaven, and of those on earth, and of those under the earth, and that every tongue should confess that Jesus Christ is Lord, to the glory of God the Father (Philippians 2: 9-11)

Secondly, we have a reminder of life's fragility. We never know when a serious accident or disease will overtake us. We can take all the necessary safety precautions, but even the wisdom of humanity may not be enough. With all our efforts, we still have to face unexpected dangers. Storms of life are always around the corner.

Thirdly, we see that the disciples were able to call Jesus their Master but were filled with terror at the prospect of drowning. Even the best of Christians can experience extreme fear when in extreme circumstances. Jesus asks us, "Where is your faith?" Or, "Where is that measure of your faith?"

The Christian church is in more danger in certain parts of the world than it has ever been. Christians are being persecuted, abused, tortured and killed. Much prayer and support is needed for this time of great trial. We do not know where the hammer will fall next. We do know that whatever we may face on this earth, we are close to God's heart and safe in eternity. One of Jesus' repeated sayings in the Gospels was, "Do not be afraid."

Finally, we note that although the storm had ceased, the disciples were terror-stricken. The cause had changed from fear of the raging storm to the realization that they were in the presence of one who was even more powerful than the elements. In the Bible, when people came into the presence of God, the prime emotion was fear. John, the writer of Revelation, experienced such an event in his old age:

And when I saw Him, I fell at His feet as dead. But He laid His right hand on me, saying to me "Do not be afraid; I am the First and the Last. I am He who lives, and was dead, and behold, I am alive forevermore. Amen. And I have the keys of Hades and of Death. (Revelation 1: 17-18)

We have a wonderful, kind, loving, all-powerful God.

Luke 8:26-39

26 Then they sailed to the country of the Gadarenes, which is opposite Galilee. **27** And when He stepped out on the land, there met Him a certain man from the city who had demons for a long time. And he wore no clothes, nor did he live in a house but in the tombs. **28** When he saw Jesus, he cried out, fell down before Him, and with a loud voice said, "What have I to do with You, Jesus, Son of the Most High God? I beg You, do not torment me!" **29** For He had commanded the unclean spirit to come out of the man. For it had often seized him, and he was kept under guard, bound with chains and shackles; and he broke the bonds and was driven by the demon into the wilderness. **30** Jesus asked him, saying, "What is your name?" And he said, "Legion," because many demons had entered him. **31** And they begged Him that He would not command them to go out into the abyss. **32** Now a herd of many swine was feeding there on the mountain. So they begged Him that He would permit them to enter them. And He permitted them. **33** Then the demons went out of the man and entered the swine, and the herd ran violently down the steep place into the lake and drowned. **34** When those who fed *them* saw what had happened, they fled and told *it* in the city and in the country. **35** Then they went out to see what had happened, and came to Jesus, and found the man from whom the demons had departed, sitting at the feet of Jesus, clothed and in his right mind. And they were afraid. **36** They also who had seen *it* told them by what means he who had been demon-possessed was healed. **37** Then the whole multitude of the surrounding region of the Gadarenes asked Him to depart from them, for they were seized with great fear. And He got into the boat and returned. **38** Now the man from whom the demons had departed begged Him that he might be with Him. But Jesus sent him away, saying, **39** "Return to your own house, and tell what great things God has done for you." And he went his way and proclaimed throughout the whole city what great things Jesus had done for him.

In this passage, Jesus and His band of disciples travelled in a few small boats across the lake. During that journey, Jesus calmed a storm, and then they landed on Gentile territory. There, Jesus confronted a demon-possessed man.

This poor man had been possessed by many demons and some commentators put the figure at over 2000. Whatever the number, this man's life, brain and personality had been completely destroyed.

He was naked, in chains, and wandering around tombs of the dead, thus indicating the man's preoccupation with death. He terrorised, and because he caused mayhem and havoc in the neighbourhood, he was driven out into the desert.

His life was so completely taken over by this demonic process that every aspect of his life was deviated. If we take all the Gospel accounts of this episode together, he preferred to be naked rather than clothed, and he preferred to live amongst the tombs of the dead rather than the houses of the living. He did not try to preserve his body, but inflicted it with self-harm. Instead of having a peaceable nature, he was violent continually.

Jesus exorcized the demons, and in the performance of the deed, the demons were sent into a herd of hundreds of pigs, which in turn, careered down the hillside and into the lake, never to be seen again.

Now the modern mind might consider that this was unfair on the pig farmers and certainly to the pigs. However, what this story does illustrate is the massive power of Satan and the radical and completed nature of the treatment.

What we need to remember is this: Jesus throughout His ministry confronted evil, demons and Satan.

On the cross, He was victorious over the devil. Why? because Jesus had accomplished all that was needful to secure our salvation:

And you, being dead in your trespasses…, He has made alive together with Him, having forgiven you all trespasses, having wiped out the handwriting of requirements that was against us, which was contrary to us. And He has taken it out of the way, having nailed it to the cross. Having disarmed principalities and powers, He made a public spectacle of them, triumphing over them in it. (Colossians 2: 13-15)

In rising from the dead, Jesus conquered death, thus thwarting the devil's evil designs. Satan causes death and pollution. Jesus brings life, health and peace.

The final part of this story shows the reaction of many to Jesus Christ. The people of the town wanted Jesus to leave them. GO AWAY! They were unmoved by this man's cure. They would rather have a mad man, than a healed man. They preferred their idols and occult practices to the wholesome and gentle reign of a Saviour.

The passage states that the man was calm, dressed and in His right mind. It is sad that some symptoms of mental illness can have religious overtones. However, we can be assured that conversion to Christ is not a sign of madness but an indication of sanity.

Incidentally, the man wanted to stay with Jesus, but Jesus commissioned him to be the first missionary, to a non-Jewish country!

He went around all the local towns telling them about Jesus. It is interesting to note that north of this area was the ancient city of Damascus. As we note from Acts, Damascus was one of the first cities to form a Christian church, and that church welcomed a most unexpected convert, the Apostle Paul.

Luke 8:40-56

40 So it was, when Jesus returned, that the multitude welcomed Him, for they were all waiting for Him. **41** And behold, there came a man named Jairus, and he was a ruler of the synagogue. And he fell down at Jesus' feet and begged Him to come to his house, **42** for he had an only daughter about twelve years of age, and she was dying. But as He went, the multitudes thronged Him. **43** Now a woman, having a flow of blood for twelve years, who had spent all her livelihood on physicians and could not be healed by any, **44** came from behind and touched the border of His garment. And immediately her flow of blood stopped. **45** And Jesus said, "Who touched Me?" When all denied it, Peter and those with him said, "Master, the multitudes throng and press You, and You say, 'Who touched Me?'" **46** But Jesus said, "Somebody touched Me, for I perceived power going out from Me." **47** Now when the woman saw that she was not hidden, she came trembling; and falling down before Him, she declared to Him in the presence of all the people the reason she had touched Him and how she was healed immediately. **48** And He said to her, "Daughter, be of good cheer; your faith has made you well. Go in peace." **49** While He was still speaking, someone came from the ruler of the synagogue's *house*, saying to him, "Your daughter is dead. Do not trouble the Teacher." **50** But when Jesus heard *it*, He answered him, saying, "Do not be afraid; only believe, and she will be made well." **51** When He came into the house, He permitted no one to go in except Peter, James, and John, and the father and mother of the girl. **52** Now all wept and mourned for her; but He said, "Do not weep; she is not dead, but sleeping." **53** And they ridiculed Him, knowing that she was dead. **54** But He put them all outside, took her by the hand and called, saying, "Little girl, arise." **55** Then her spirit returned, and she arose immediately. And He commanded that she be given *something* to eat. **56** And her parents were astonished, but He charged them to tell no one what had happened.

Jesus returned to the other side of the lake, back to His main centre of Galilee ministry. There a crowd was waiting.

It is worth noticing how accessible Jesus was. Not only that, He is available, He is interruptible, and He is approachable. Unlike so many modern famous people, He was not holed out in some five star hotel in an executive suite on the tenth floor with a group of guards and administrators preventing any access. He was there in the street, on the lakeside, in the fields, in the hills, amongst the people whom He taught and healed. In fact, some have even gone as far to suggest that disease was virtually wiped out in that part of Israel. I know that doctors and other similar people have been noted to be aloof, but not Jesus.

Waiting for Him was a man named Jairus who was desperate and beside himself with worry. Jairus was the senior man in the local synagogue, perhaps a Pharisee. He knew all about the fact that the religious establishment were highly critical, and wanted to do away with Jesus. He might previously have been a seething critic himself. But something happened which changed all of that. His lovely twelve-year old daughter, on the verge of womanhood, was sick and dying. He threw himself at the feet of Jesus. It was something you only did to a King or to God. He pleaded with Jesus to come and heal his daughter. Jesus agreed immediately, and set off with him to the house. All around Him, people were heaving and shoving. There was no doubt a lot of talking, shouting, the general cacophony of an excited crowd.

We are then introduced to a needy woman. She was suffering from bleeding, what doctors call menorrhagia, which started twelve years previously, around the same time as Jairus' daughter's birth. She was designated as unclean. She should not have been there. She was not allowed to touch anyone, including her own family. She was thrown out of the synagogue.

She was out of fellowship, and had no access to the word of God, and no admittance to the reading of Scripture.

Luke the physician says that she could not be cured. Mark, describing the same incident, says that she had spent all that she had on doctors but could not be healed of any. Medical fees have always been expensive. Mark's Gospel appears to take a very dim view of it. Jesus charged nothing.

Medical care is expensive. The modern treatment for this lady's condition would be a hysterectomy.

The cost of a private hysterectomy at a private hospital in London is in the order of £8000. In the rest of the country, it is less than that. The overall average is £6000. This woman had spent much. But, she thought that if she could touch Jesus, then she would be healed.

She did and she was. Then we have this wonderful insight into the divine nature of Jesus.

He stopped and paused, "Who touched Me?"

He felt power had gone out of Him. When God deals with us in some way, divine power goes out from Him.

The woman came and knelt before Him and told her story. He addressed her in a warm tone, "Daughter." In the Gospels, Jesus addressed no other woman in that way.

"Your faith has healed or saved you." Jesus healed people who may not have become believers. This lady received both healing and salvation.

Meanwhile, Jairus was becoming even more agitated and desperate. This interruption meant time was running out on his daughter. The news came that she was dead.

Jesus responded and urged Jairus to, "Keep on believing." (v.50) Now when anyone died in that culture, burial took place within three hours or so. So when they arrived at the house, the funeral was underway.

In the United Kingdom, funerals are hushed, solemn occasions. In first century Israel, they were loud and explosive with emotion. Hired mourners would wail and weep. Pipes would sound their loud shrill, dissonant tones. He took three disciples with the parents into the house and said, "She is not dead!" The mourners laughed, and this demonstrated their utter insincerity. (v.53)

All became quiet, and He touched the girl by the hand and she sat up. This was a raising from the dead. The supernatural is then wonderfully combined with the natural. The girl had not eaten for ages. "So give her something to eat." (v.55)

We learn from this passage that these were people in great need.

If anyone admits that they are in need, then God is not remote and unknowable. In the Old Testament, there were detailed rules and procedures as to how God should be approached. The overriding story is one of utter holiness. But we do have glimpses, when we are told that Moses talked with God as a man talks with his friend.

In the New Testament, Paul urged us to call out, "Abba, Father," (Romans 8: 15) or perhaps more accurately translated, "My dear Father." These are two important aspects of the same thing, His holiness and His love. In fact, when truly considered, it is impossible to have an all-loving God without also being a holy God who cannot contemplate sin and whose judgments are wise and just.

Luke 9:1-9

1 Then He called His twelve disciples together and gave them power and authority over all demons, and to cure diseases. **2** He sent them to preach the kingdom of God and to heal the sick. **3** And He said to them, "Take nothing for the journey, neither staffs nor bag nor bread nor money; and do not have two tunics apiece. **4** "Whatever house you enter, stay there, and from there depart. **5** And whoever will not receive you, when you go out of that city, shake off the very dust from your feet as a testimony against them." **6** So they departed and went through the towns, preaching the gospel and healing everywhere. **7** Now Herod the tetrarch heard of all that was done by Him; and he was perplexed, because it was said by some that John had risen from the dead, **8** and by some that Elijah had appeared, and by others that one of the old prophets had risen again. **9** Herod said, "John I have beheaded, but who is this of whom I hear such things?" So he sought to see Him.

In this passage, we see the increasing influence of Jesus' earthly ministry. The disciples were still in a learning stage and yet they were sent out with significant responsibilities. It is good to encourage young Christians to share their faith. From this passage it is possible to see a number of effects.

Firstly, we see God at work in the changing of lives and the healing of lives. Although nowadays we do not see the same extent of demon possession as was then, many lives are ruled by Satan in the form of addictions and polluted living. Many show a captive personality in their coldness and utter resistance to the Gospel. Many are made sick by their lifestyles.

It is amazing to see lives changed by the Gospel and put on the right track. Sometimes the conversion is rapid; sometimes it takes place after years of patience and prayer.

Secondly, we are not told the content of their message, but we do know that they proclaimed the kingdom of God. This is the place where Jesus reigns. It is within the heart and mind and is about our ultimate loyalty and allegiance. Jesus spoke often about the kingdom in His teaching and parables.

Much ink has been spilt in subsequent centuries in argument and discussion about the meaning of the kingdom of God. Is it now or in the future? To what extent can we reproduce it on earth? Suffice to say that it begins at the cross where we realise our need of forgiveness and that Jesus has paid the price and has borne our just punishment on Himself. Peter, one of those twelve wrote years later:

For to this you were called, because Christ also suffered for us, leaving us an example, that you should follow His steps: "Who committed no sin, Nor was deceit found in His mouth"; who, when He was reviled, did not revile in return; when He suffered, He did not threaten, but committed Himself to Him who judges righteously; who Himself bore our sins in His own body on the tree, that we, having died to sins, might live for righteousness—by whose stripes you were healed. For you were like sheep going astray, but have now returned to the Shepherd and Overseer of your souls. (1 Peter 2:21-25)

Thirdly, we see the absence of baggage, money, food for the journey. In doing so, they were taught to trust God for everything. In their journeys in the book of Acts, they did carry money and some extras, but they never lost their sense of trust. There were people who received them and there were those who refused. It is a picture of response to the Gospel that has been present ever since.

The final verses of this passage introduce us to Herod Antipas. They show a contrast between the kingdom proclaimed by Jesus and the twelve and that of Herod. In one, evil is confronted and dealt with, the sick are healed and cared for, and the good news is preached. In the other, Herod presided over a corrupt, louche, murderous, superstitious administration that cared little about the general population. One had little in the way of physical resources. The other prided itself in its ability to run lavish and drunken parties. Herod and his advisers had no idea what was going on in the region of Galilee. Herod's mind was tickled by the preaching of John the Baptist. His conscience was aroused after he had beheaded John. He expressed interest in Jesus, but not to the extent that it might change his corrupt and dissolute ways. Later Jesus described him as, "that Fox." (Luke 13: 32).

There are always people who will be interested in Jesus and religion. Comparatively few, however, wish to enter His kingdom.

Luke 9:10-17

10 And the apostles, when they had returned, told Him all that they had done. Then He took them and went aside privately into a deserted place belonging to the city called Bethsaida. **11** But when the multitudes knew *it*, they followed Him; and He received them and spoke to them about the kingdom of God, and healed those who had need of healing. **12** When the day began to wear away, the twelve came and said to Him, "Send the multitude away, that they may go into the surrounding towns and country, and lodge and get provisions; for we are in a deserted place here." **13** But He said to them, "You give them something to eat." And they said, "We have no more than five loaves and two fish, unless we go and buy food for all these people." **14** For there were about five thousand men. Then He said to His disciples, "Make them sit down in groups of fifty." **15** And they did so, and made them all sit down. **16** Then He took the five loaves and the two fish, and looking up to heaven, He blessed and broke them, and gave *them* to the disciples to set before the multitude. **17** So they all ate and were filled, and twelve baskets of the leftover fragments were taken up by them.

This passage emphasizes the need for busy people to have times of quiet and refreshment. God's work is God's work and although we are to be active in work, whether in employment or otherwise, the future is not dependent on us. Many a Christian has come to a grinding halt because of failure to achieve a proper life-work balance. We are also reminded of the need to be even-tempered and flexible in the face of interruptions.

The "Feeding of the Five thousand", is the only miracle except the resurrection that is recorded in all four Gospels. This gives emphasis to its veracity and also its symbolism.

Many commentators have suggested that the presence of Jesus made people more kind and considerate towards others, even those who otherwise were strangers. It was a miracle of sharing rather than a miracle of creation. Such views are not those of the Gospel writers themselves. They were convinced and sought to convince their readers that a great miracle and sign took place on that crowded day.

It was a multiplier act of creation. The one who made the earth was able to produce cooked fishes and bread in an instant.

The question arises as to who was aware that a miracle had taken place. From reading the other Gospels, it appears that the disciples and some others knew. John indicates that there were those who wished to make Jesus king by force, (John 6:14-15). Probably, there were thousands who somehow thought that the appearance of food just happened, like children who are unaware of their parents' efforts until they too become adults.

Many believe creation is like that. Given the right ingredients everything will fall into place. It may take millions of years, but somehow, everything will evolve by chance. Anyone who casts any criticism on this view comes under severe censure, and may even risk a loss of job.

Fraser Munro summed up a critique of macro-evolution as follows:

The existence of a painting demands a painter. The existence of a sculpture demands the existence of a sculptor. The existence of a book demands the existence of an author. The existence of creation demands the existence of a creator. (Fraser Munro, *The Folly of Atheism* (John Ritchie Ltd, 2013) p. 5)

Some commentators have pointed out that the "Feeding of the five thousand" was an earthly foretaste of the joyful heavenly divine banquet. (Rev 19:7-9) What we do know is that the Lord Jesus was and will be present at both.

Many have a low view of Christ; He is a mere teacher, prophet, or healer. The Apostle Paul had no such view:

He is the image of the invisible God, the firstborn over all creation. For by Him all things were created that are in heaven and that are on earth, visible and invisible, whether thrones or dominions or principalities or powers. All things were created through Him and for Him. And He is before all things, and in Him all things consist. And He is the head of the body, the church, who is the beginning, the firstborn from the dead, that in all things He may have the preeminence. For it pleased the Father that in Him all the fullness should dwell, and by Him to reconcile all things to Himself, by Him, whether things on earth or things in heaven, having made peace through the blood of His cross. (Colossians 1: 15-20)

The passage states, (v.17) that all of those who ate were satisfied. The Gospel satisfies humanity's deepest needs. Since the feeding of the five thousand, millions have fed on Christ by faith. Jesus referred to Himself as "The Bread of Life." (John 6: 35) We must pray that many more will be partakers of this true bread.

Luke 9:18-27

18 And it happened, as He was alone praying, *that* His disciples joined Him, and He asked them, saying, "Who do the crowds say that I am?" **19** So they answered and said, "John the Baptist, but some *say* Elijah; and others *say* that one of the old prophets has risen again." **20** He said to them, "But who do you say that I am?" Peter answered and said, "The Christ of God." **21** And He strictly warned and commanded them to tell this to no one, **22** saying, "The Son of Man must suffer many things, and be rejected by the elders and chief priests and scribes, and be killed, and be raised the third day." **23** Then He said to *them* all, "If anyone desires to come after Me, let him deny himself, and take up his cross daily, and follow Me. **24** For whoever desires to save his life will lose it, but whoever loses his life for My sake will save it. **25** For what profit is it to a man if he gains the whole world, and is himself destroyed or lost? **26** For whoever is ashamed of Me and My words, of him the Son of Man will be ashamed when He comes in His *own* glory, and *in His* Father's, and of the holy angels. **27** But I tell you truly, there are some standing here who shall not taste death till they see the kingdom of God."

The passage introduces us to the importance of private prayer. If Jesus spent time in prayer so should we. It is often the most neglected practice in Christianity. We spend much time sleeping, eating, working and entertaining ourselves, but insufficient time in prayer.

Today all the big organizations spend significant effort in market research and opinion polls. They are very sophisticated tools in the modern world. Even so, they are still sometimes proved to be wrong.

Jesus sought to know the opinion of the masses in order to teach the disciples. It was not necessary to employ detailed sampling methods to evaluate percentages – it was sufficient to know some say this and some say that. The crowds' verdicts were limited by their own expectations. They had been taught and may even have read about the prophets. They had heard John the Baptist, and there was a widespread belief in the possibility of resurrection. Their verdict on Jesus was a diverse mixture.

Then came the key question. "But what about you, who do you say I am?" (v. 20)

Peter's answer was immediate and sounds rushed, and he no doubt spoke for them all. Peter had seen everything about Jesus at close quarters. In a comparatively short time, he had witnessed much. As they walked through the countryside, and perhaps whilst awake during the night, he must have experienced a mass of thoughts going round and round in his mind as he considered who this extraordinary Jesus was.

"The Christ of God" indicated their belief that Jesus was a great deliverer and also the promised Messiah.

Jesus then told them not to tell anyone because there were so many false notions as to the nature of a Messiah. Jesus, as in other places, then referred to Himself as, "The Son of Man." This is more mysterious than saying, "This man," or, "This weak mortal man," as the Aramaic words may suggest. It is also a divine title, expressed in the book of Daniel. (Daniel 7: 13-14)

Jesus went on to describe what the Messiah of Israel had to do. The task was both appalling and shocking.

Scores of men in the restive, rebellious area of Galilee had been executed by the most terrible of Roman punishments. Yet the purpose of the Messiah was to preach, heal and usher in a new kingdom. All this is dependent on Jesus' death on a cross. It took some time before they understood that Jesus, the Messiah of God, would suffer and rise again for the salvation of the world. It was also unpalatable to be told that the path of each follower was that of the cross. To take up one's cross is to identify oneself with the fact that Jesus is our sacrifice for sin. It means that I acknowledge that sacrifice daily, whatever the cost.

In the end it is the only wise option. Why lose in eternity when the cost on earth is to follow Christ? There may be inconvenience or even trouble and persecution. There will be diseases and disasters, but we need to realise even with great difficulty that these are nothing compared with the peace of God that comes through knowing Christ.

Verses 26 and 27 remind us of the second coming when all will have to acknowledge the Lordship of Christ. The final phrase is something of a mystery:

But I tell you truly, there are some standing here who shall not taste death till they see the kingdom of God.

It is reasonable to think that this prophecy was fulfilled a week or so later, when three disciples witnessed or "beheld" His glory. (John 1: 14)

Luke 9:28-45

28 Now it came to pass, about eight days after these sayings, that He took Peter, John, and James and went up on the mountain to pray. **29** As He prayed, the appearance of His face was altered, and His robe *became* white *and* glistening. **30** And behold, two men talked with Him, who were Moses and Elijah, **31** who appeared in glory and spoke of His decease which He was about to accomplish at Jerusalem. **32** But Peter and those with him were heavy with sleep; and when they were fully awake, they saw His glory and the two men who stood with Him. **33** Then it happened, as they were parting from Him, *that* Peter said to Jesus, "Master, it is good for us to be here; and let us make three tabernacles: one for You, one for Moses, and one for Elijah"—not knowing what he said. **34** While he was saying this, a cloud came and overshadowed them; and they were fearful as they entered the cloud. **35** And a voice came out of the cloud, saying, "This is My beloved Son. Hear Him!" **36** When the voice had ceased, Jesus was found alone. But they kept quiet, and told no one in those days any of the things they had seen. **37** Now it happened on the next day, when they had come down from the mountain, that a great multitude met Him. **38** Suddenly a man from the multitude cried out, saying, "Teacher, I implore You, look on my son, for he is my only child. **39** And behold, a spirit seizes him, and he suddenly cries out; it convulses him so that he foams *at the mouth;* and it departs from him with great difficulty, bruising him. **40** So I implored Your disciples to cast it out, but they could not." **41** Then Jesus answered and said, "O faithless and perverse generation, how long shall I be with you and bear with you? Bring your son here." **42** And as he was still coming, the demon threw him down and convulsed *him.* Then Jesus rebuked the unclean spirit, healed the child, and gave him back to his father. **43** And they were all amazed at the majesty of God. But while everyone marveled at all the things which Jesus did, He said to His disciples, **44** "Let these words sink down into your ears, for the Son of Man is about to be betrayed into the hands of men." **45** But they did not understand this saying, and it was hidden from them so that they did not perceive it; and they were afraid to ask Him about this saying.

Jesus went up into a mountain to pray. He took His inner circle with Him, Peter, John and James. These three accompanied Jesus to the house of Jairus when Jesus raised his daughter, and again in the Garden of Gethsemane shortly before Jesus's arrest.

The disciples became sleepy, perhaps tired with exertion and worry, but Jesus' appearance began to change. His face shone like the sun, and He shone through His clothes, which in turn looked like lightening.

Now, this was a preview of the second coming when Christ will come in glory. Jesus talked about the "second coming" on a number of occasions, and this is what the apostles and the church would later teach. Many did then, as they do now, say, "He hasn't come yet, He is not going to come." Well these three had a glimpse of Christ in His glory.

This transfiguration, as we call it, is the most important event between the birth of Jesus and the cross of Jesus. Matthew, Mark and John referred to it. John referred to it in the first chapter of his gospel, "We beheld His glory." Peter referred to it in his second epistle, when he talks about the mountain-top experience. (2 Peter 1: 17) The experience was profound and moving.

The brightness of the light coming from Jesus' person showed His glory and deity. The light was not reflected or transferred light but emanated out of Jesus Himself. The disciples were heavy with sleep. When they woke up, they saw this amazing, wonderful sight of Jesus, and He was there talking with two great characters from the Old Testament. Once again, Jesus spoke about His death.

Then Peter decided to put in his contribution. It was a time when it would have been wise to keep quiet.

Peter often was quick to react, quick to speak. He was a case of "foot-in-mouth syndrome" when someone opens their mouth and puts their foot in it before they think. It is tongue in gear, brain in neutral. That is why it is often necessary to guard our tongue. It can cause so much hurt and misunderstanding.

He said, "Let's make three tabernacles," (v.33) or little houses, one for each one, Jesus, Moses and Elijah. Luke says that he, Peter, did not know what he was saying. He wanted this experience to go on and on. He wanted to stay in this supernatural world. Peter's words seem to indicate a kind of equality between Jesus, Moses and Elijah. There was not and there is not. It is tempting to follow the voice of a preacher or teacher, but we should only do so when it is consistent with the words of Jesus. We should respect people, but Jesus should have the highest honour.

Then normal service was soon resumed, but what a glimpse they had had of the Lord's glory.

On descent from the mountain, we see a child who was inhabited by an "unclean spirit." The physical symptoms described are similar to those of grand mal epilepsy. A generalized convulsion (grand mal) characteristically begins with a sudden loss of consciousness, a cry, a fall to the ground with stiffening and then rhythmic jerking of the head, facial muscles and limbs. There may be foaming at the mouth and biting of the tongue. Then a period of unconsciousness is followed by recovery at varying intervals. Hippocrates (c. 400 BC) wrote a treatise on epilepsy and discounted the idea that the sufferer was inhabited by a god, which was the earlier Greek thought. He considered that the illness was a condition of the brain.

It is interesting to note that Luke states that Jesus rebuked the unclean spirit and healed the child and then handed the boy back to his father. We could understand that there were three acts here around the two interconnected conditions. Both the demon possession was dealt with and the epilepsy was healed.

Jesus' exasperation with the disciples indicated the nature of their spluttering faith and their own inability to effect a cure, even though the mission a few weeks prior to that was accompanied by success. It once again demonstrates the veracity of the Gospel record. No cunningly devised fable would have put the disciples in such a bad light. It is remarkable and unfathomable that God uses even people like us to fulfil His sovereign plans.

There is a third reference to Jesus' betrayal and death. He has demonstrated His glory and healing power and yet He was prepared to empty Himself into the hands of men whose only motive was hate, and intention was harm. We remember here that Jesus was put to death by violent men but also submitted Himself to it quite voluntarily as part of God's purpose of redemption. It would only be after the resurrection that the disciples understood the meaning and significance of the cross. In the meantime they could not grasp it. Modern humanity is not alone in its failure to understand the death of Christ.

Luke 9:46-50

46 Then a dispute arose among them as to which of them would be greatest. **47** And Jesus, perceiving the thought of their heart, took a little child and set him by Him, **48** and said to them, "Whoever receives this little child in My name receives Me; and whoever receives Me receives Him who sent Me. For he who is least among you all will be great." **49** Now John answered and said, "Master, we saw someone casting out demons in Your name, and we forbade him because he does not follow with us." **50** But Jesus said to him, "Do not forbid *him,* for he who is not against us is on our side."

Here we have a number of episodes which demonstrate a deep, deep flaw in human nature and the disciples' nature, their pride.

I have often had difficulty with this one because as youngsters we were told to have a pride in our work and we heard about people being proud of their family's achievements and so on. Furthermore, I came to another conclusion that without some form of self-confidence, a teacher would not stand in front of a class, a builder would not lay a brick, a musician would not play a note, a lawyer would not deliver a brief or stand up in court, an engineer would not test a design, a doctor would not sign a prescription, and a surgeon would not make an incision.

However, this is all about self-promotion, self-absorption, self-centredness, and self-conceit, which has been deep in the psyche of humanity. In fact we have made all this into a virtue. There are me-centred ideas. We are "the self generation", and as the decades go by we have become more self-oriented and more narcissistic. Sociologists have shown this from repeated questionnaires and testing. Pride stalks everywhere.

When we become a Christian, we have a new beginning and a new heart, and yet we have pride lurking in the nooks and crannies of the human brain. We have to address it repeatedly.

We see it operate in the world, in organizations, and institutions with its power struggles and ruthless operations.

We see pride in churches. In my lifetime, because of moves connected with my job, I have attended nearly ten churches and visited many others. When pride comes to the fore, churches can become toxic.

Pride destroys unity. It ruined relationships in the church in Corinth. People were saying: "I am of Paul", "I am of Apollos", "I am of Cephas", "I am of Christ". (1 Corinthians 1:12)

Pride encourages partiality. Proud people believe that the world revolves around them. It encourages exclusivity. It is sectarian.

Pride restrains mercy. I spoke to a widowed man who had married for a second time. In a telephone conversation to his first wife's sister, he said that he had become very happy again. His wife's sister has subsequently never spoken to him.

The disciples who were in the main fishermen and artisans copied the religious leaders whose level of importance was signified by the length of tassel on their shawls, by their flowing robes, by greetings in the street, and by their title, 'rabbi'. (Luke 20: 46)

Jesus would have none of this and took a little child and placed them in front of them. Jesus said that whoever receives such a child in His name receives Him.

So what is it about a little child that we should note?

Is it that they can be a handful? No.

Is it that they are to some people "kind of cute"?

Is it that they tend to be vulnerable, trusting and dependent? Well there could be something in that.

What we have to do is to go back to 1st Century Israel.

We used to have a saying that children should be seen and not heard. In those times, not only should they not be heard, they should not even be seen!

A child's life expectancy was such that they had little or no status.

Jesus said that you have to be like that. We rely so much on our social position and status, what initials we have after our name, how much money we have, and so on.

When we come to Him we all come as sinners, and in some cases proud sinners, who need to repent, who need forgiveness, who need a new heart and attitude, who need a new love for God. It is disarming and humbling.

After showing them a child, they were still at it. They saw a man who was ministering in the name of Jesus.

The disciples asked if they should rebuke him. "After all, he is not one of us. He is not part of the in-group. He does not have our insignia. He is not from our denomination." Jesus had to correct their thinking.

Luke 9:51-62

51 Now it came to pass, when the time had come for Him to be received up, that He steadfastly set His face to go to Jerusalem, 52 and sent messengers before His face. And as they went, they entered a village of the Samaritans, to prepare for Him. 53 But they did not receive Him, because His face was *set* for the journey to Jerusalem. 54 And when His disciples James and John saw *this*, they said, "Lord, do You want us to command fire to come down from heaven and consume them, just as Elijah did?" 55 But He turned and rebuked them, and said, "You do not know what manner of spirit you are of. 56 For the Son of Man did not come to destroy men's lives but to save *them*." And they went to another village. 57 Now it happened as they journeyed on the road, *that* someone said to Him, "Lord, I will follow You wherever You go." 58 And Jesus said to him, "Foxes have holes and birds of the air *have* nests, but the Son of Man has nowhere to lay *His* head." 59 Then He said to another, "Follow Me." But he said, "Lord, let me first go and bury my father." 60 Jesus said to him, "Let the dead bury their own dead, but you go and preach the kingdom of God." 61 And another also said, "Lord, I will follow You, but let me first go *and* bid them farewell who are at my house." 62 But Jesus said to him, "No one, having put his hand to the plow, and looking back, is fit for the kingdom of God."

Jesus, having spoken on more than one occasion about the cross, set His face to go to Jerusalem. Unusually, they began on the direct route and came to a Samaritan village. The reason why it was unusual was because the Jews and the Samaritans loathed each other.

"Should we bring down fire?" This was reminiscent of an event in the life of Elijah.

It was pride again. Yet, a few years later, this very group, the Samaritans, would become Christians or Messianic believers, under the ministry of Philip the evangelist. Peter and John would come and lay hands on them. It is easy to condemn people, people of different political persuasion or party, or others who may or may not be respectable. But they are our mission field. A Christian should not be a proud, highly moralised being, issuing edicts from a superior position. As someone once described it, "a Christian is a beggar, who tells other beggars where they can obtain bread."

This passage is instructive because we see Jesus' prohibition of violence in the cause of Christian mission. Atheist critics have often condemned the church for events such as the Inquisition and the history of religious wars. Such things, it must be admitted, have been far more than a scandal. However, we all need to be humble on this issue and point out that atheist regimes, from the French revolution through to North Korea, via Stalin and Mao, have far exceeded the persecution dealt out by people who have called themselves religious. These regimes together have killed their tens of millions. There are no depths to the crimes of humanity.

The remaining verses of this chapter deal with the cost of following Jesus and our response. At this point in Jesus' ministry, He still commanded enormous popularity amongst tens of thousands of ordinary people. He healed many, taught with great authority and demonstrated supreme communication skills. He had what modern journalists call, 'momentum'. So it would be natural for enthusiasts to have part of the action.

Many of us in evangelism are reluctant to give any account of the hardships of true Christianity. We neglect to indicate the pressures that will inevitably fall on the new convert. There will be rejection by friends and ridicule from others. In parts of the world there is loss of home, torture and even loss of life. Evangelists can so easily fall into the role of a salesman rather than a wise and loving presenter of the Gospel.

Others, Jesus called to follow Him. These episodes indicate the wholehearted nature and necessary commitment of true discipleship. Jesus comes before family.

At this point it should be stated that the replies given to Jesus are not as reasonable as they might have sounded. In the first instance it is possible that the man's father was not yet dead. In that part of the world, burial was within a day of death, and the man would not have been in any position to be out on the road and receiving the Lord's invitation.

In the second instance, the goodbye may not have been a rapid occurrence but a long drawn-out process lasting months.

It needs to be said that families have often discouraged younger members from stepping out in their quest for independence. Such stifling atmospheres are discouraging and can lead to embitterment. (Colossians 3: 21)

Finally, it needs to be stated that we all have responsibilities towards our families. Our responsibility is outlined in the Ten Commandments. There is a balance to be struck between independence and honouring our parents and caring for the needs of close relatives.

Luke 10:1-12

1 After these things the Lord appointed seventy others also, and sent them two by two before His face into every city and place where He Himself was about to go. **2** Then He said to them, "The harvest truly *is* great, but the laborers *are* few; therefore pray the Lord of the harvest to send out laborers into His harvest. **3** Go your way; behold, I send you out as lambs among wolves. **4** Carry neither money bag, knapsack, nor sandals; and greet no one along the road. **5** But whatever house you enter, first say, 'Peace to this house.' **6** And if a son of peace is there, your peace will rest on it; if not, it will return to you. **7** And remain in the same house, eating and drinking such things as they give, for the laborer is worthy of his wages. Do not go from house to house. **8** Whatever city you enter, and they receive you, eat such things as are set before you. **9** And heal the sick there, and say to them, 'The kingdom of God has come near to you.' **10** But whatever city you enter, and they do not receive you, go out into its streets and say, **11** 'The very dust of your city which clings to us we wipe off against you. Nevertheless know this, that the kingdom of God has come near you.' **12** But I say to you that it will be more tolerable in that Day for Sodom than for that city."

One of the first comments that Jesus makes is that the harvest is plentiful. In other words, there are still people out there and around us who are to become Christian. In the West, there are large numbers of people who are very ignorant of the news about Jesus.

In China there are around 80 million Christians. However, a few years ago I was informed by a knowledgeable China watcher that there are more people in China who have never heard of Christ, than live in the whole of Africa.

Some time ago the boss of Coca Cola said it was his ambition during the next few years to ensure that everyone on the planet had heard of his product. I think his ambition either has been or very soon will be achieved.

Do we want everyone hear about Jesus? Jesus tells us that such labourers are few. I like this remark by an old preacher, "Colleges may train, bishops may ordain and patrons or elders may appoint, but it is God who truly calls and sends out labourers."

There are pew-filler Christians, briefcase ministers, but the number of Gospel labourers is few.

Because they are so few, our Lord, firstly, urges us to pray for labourers or people prepared to put up with hardship in order to share the Gospel. We do not all have gifts of speech or the necessary finance, or confidence but we can all have evangelism as a priority and pray for labourers, labourers who do not moan about their circumstances and eat what is offered. (v. 8)

I heard on the radio recently that Britain is a country that complains. That should not be the first impression of a Christian.

As the seventy went from house to house and town to town there were two responses. One from a man or son of peace, and that is acceptance. The other is rejection. Today, we have lot of rejection.

The world around us is like a tale of two cities. This is similar to a description in the book of Revelation. (Revelation 18-21)

The one city is Jerusalem, not like the one Jesus wept over, but the heavenly Jerusalem, which accepts the reign of God. It is a picture of the kingdom of God.

The other city is Babylon, where God is not accepted. There is self-promotion, self-rule, self-aggrandisement, and self-seeking. There is party spirit, anger and rejection of all things pertaining to God. It is a city where there are "fifty shades of grey."

Yet, the Bible says that in that city instead of freedom, there is a form of captivity. "Whoever commits sin is a slave of sin." (John 8:34)

William Penn, one of the founding fathers of America, said this, "Men must be governed by God or they will be ruled by tyrants."

Jesus says to those in that city of Babylon, "Come out from among them and be separate!" (2 Corinthians 6:17)

Now some have taken this as a requirement for total withdrawal. That is not really the case. God wants you to be His man or woman in that workplace, or if you wish to be a member, in that society, in that sports club or wherever. But He does want you to live a "separated walk."

In other words, people can tell by your speech, actions and attitudes that there is something different about you. Your speech betrays you!

When a Jew had returned from abroad, before planting his feet on home ground, he would shake the dust off his feet and clothes. It was a symbol of rejection of Gentile territory. The poignant implication in this passage is that those who accept Jesus are grafted into and part of the true Israel.

Luke 10:13-24

13 "Woe to you, Chorazin! Woe to you, Bethsaida! For if the mighty works which were done in you had been done in Tyre and Sidon, they would have repented long ago, sitting in sackcloth and ashes. **14** But it will be more tolerable for Tyre and Sidon at the judgment than for you. **15** And you, Capernaum, who are exalted to heaven, will be brought down to Hades. **16** He who hears you hears Me, he who rejects you rejects Me, and he who rejects Me rejects Him who sent Me." **17** Then the seventy returned with joy, saying, "Lord, even the demons are subject to us in Your name." **18** And He said to them, "I saw Satan fall like lightning from heaven. **19** Behold, I give you the authority to trample on serpents and scorpions, and over all the power of the enemy, and nothing shall by any means hurt you. **20** Nevertheless do not rejoice in this, that the spirits are subject to you, but rather rejoice because your names are written in heaven." **21** In that hour Jesus rejoiced in the Spirit and said, "I thank You, Father, Lord of heaven and earth, that You have hidden these things from *the* wise and prudent and revealed them to babes. Even so, Father, for so it seemed good in Your sight. **22** All things have been delivered to Me by My Father, and no one knows who the Son is except the Father, and who the Father is except the Son, and *the one* to whom the Son wills to reveal *Him.*" **23** Then He turned to *His* disciples and said privately, "Blessed *are* the eyes which see the things you see; **24** for I tell you that many prophets and kings have desired to see what you see, and have not seen *it,* and to hear what you hear, and have not heard *it.*"

We move onto a hard section of the passage, which involves judgment on various towns.

Great signs were performed in these towns.

Bethsaida, on the shores of Galilee, was where Peter, Andrew and Philip came from. It means "the house of fish." It was where Jesus healed a blind man and near to the feeding of the five thousand.

Capernaum was nearby and a centre of Jesus' ministry. It was the location of Peter's house. It was where Jesus performed signs and miracles. These involved notable persons in the town, a centurion, Jairus and a nobleman. We could make a significant list of all that Jesus did. What a privilege! Chorazin is a place which is only mentioned here and in Matthew. Yet in spite of all this wonder and ministry, Jesus pronounces woe to them.

It is as if they had become totally hardened to Jesus almost by familiarity. It happens time and time again.

David Pawson the well-known Bible teacher said this:

I tremble for some people who listen Sunday after Sunday to the Word of God. If you do not believe, what is the word doing to you? So we must remember that those who refuse God's Word are not left neutral, nor left in the same condition so that a year later they can come back and listen. Something has happened- they become calloused, harder, more difficult to persuade.

There is much truth in this, although I do know of people who have been converted in their seventies after years of church attendance.

These towns were not struck down by a lightening bolt, neither were they flattened by the Romans as Jerusalem and other towns were in AD 70. They just withered away and became archaeological sites.

Jesus compared them with Tyre and Sidon. Later in Acts, Paul visited both of these cities and shared fellowship with believers. We never hear the same about these fishing towns.

The return of the seventy was accompanied by much excitement.

"I saw Satan fall like lightening from heaven," referred to the success of the seventy, but there is more.

When we become Christians we can trample on all those symbols of evil and not be harmed. There is no need to say, "Touch wood," or throw salt over your shoulder or consult horoscopes or be scared by an allegedly haunted house.

But be glad that your names are written in heaven. (v.20)

The devil still is active but he is overcome.

One preacher has compared the situation to the last months of

World War 2. It was clear the Nazi armies were defeated, but there was still some more to do. Their fate was sealed; it was a matter of time. So it is with Satan. His fate is sealed.

Now we move from judgment to salvation, from woe to joy.

Jesus was full of joy in or through the Holy Spirit. (v. 21)

Christianity contains all the emotions – contentment, happiness, sorrow, weeping, and disappointment, except revenge, and malice, and fits of rage. Here we see Jesus full of joy because some whom the world would not regard as particularly significant had become believers. Heaven is a place of joy because people are becoming Christians all over the world. Jesus' joy is a joy He wishes to give to us.

It is not to the most powerful, not to the most intellectual, not to the most intelligent, not to the wisest, but to "babes", and those you might least expect. His arms are wider than we think.

Finally, we need to realize what a privileged people we are.

Jesus wanted His hearers to know that they had seen and come to know more than the great characters of the Old Testament.

Do you believe that you are special? Of everything in the Universe, you are unique, and if you have come to God in faith, the whole of Heaven is overjoyed because of what you have done.

Luke 10:25-42

25 And behold, a certain lawyer stood up and tested Him, saying, "Teacher, what shall I do to inherit eternal life?" 26 He said to him, "What is written in the law? What is your reading *of it?*" 27 So he answered and said, " 'You shall love the LORD your God with all your heart, with all your soul, with all your strength, and with all your mind,' and 'your neighbor as yourself.'" 28 And He said to him, "You have answered rightly; do this and you will live." 29 But he, wanting to justify himself, said to Jesus, "And who is my neighbor?" 30 Then Jesus answered and said: "A certain *man* went down from Jerusalem to Jericho, and fell among thieves, who stripped him of his clothing, wounded *him,* and departed, leaving *him* half dead. 31 Now by chance a certain priest came down that road. And when he saw him, he passed by on the other side. 32 Likewise a Levite, when he arrived at the place, came and looked, and passed by on the other side. 33 But a certain Samaritan, as he journeyed, came where he was. And when he saw him, he had compassion. 34 So he went to *him* and bandaged his wounds, pouring on oil and wine; and he set him on his own animal, brought him to an inn, and took care of him. 35 On the next day, when he departed, he took out two denarii, gave *them* to the innkeeper, and said to him, 'Take care of him; and whatever more you spend, when I come again, I will repay you.' 36 So which of these three do you think was neighbor to him who fell among the thieves?" 37 And he said, "He who showed mercy on him." Then Jesus said to him, "Go and do likewise." 38 Now it happened as they went that He entered a certain village; and a certain woman named Martha welcomed Him into her house. 39 And she had a sister called Mary, who also sat at Jesus' feet and heard His word. 40 But Martha was distracted with much serving, and she approached Him and said, "Lord, do You not care that my sister has left me to serve alone? Therefore tell her to help me." 41 And Jesus answered and said to her, "Martha, Martha, you are worried and troubled about many things. 42 But one thing is needed, and Mary has chosen that good part, which will not be taken away from her."

Wherever Christianity is taught in the world, the parable of the Good Samaritan will be heard. Sadly, even amongst the educated in Britain, this challenging story is being forgotten.

Whilst coming to the end of a long surgical operation, I recounted the story to those present in the operating theatre. These were people who were diligent and hard-working, whom I both liked and admired. Of the seven present, only three could recall that they had heard the story before. One of the three was a Muslim.

The parable is part of a response to a lawyer's tempting and perhaps insincere question, "Teacher, what shall I do to inherit eternal life?"

Our western idea of eternal life is life forever with God, even through the interruption of death. It may not be quite the same idea as was held by this lawyer and first century Judaism. Many scholars have thought hard about this one, and the prevalent view is the lawyer meant, "life in the age to come." However, it is reasonable to think in those days as today that there was a sense of the desire for total safety even through death and eternity. The prevalent belief in the resurrection exemplifies this point.

Jesus' reply asked the lawyer about his reading of the Law. Jesus did not ask about man's teaching or that of the rabbis and tradition, but what does God teach? To love God and love our neighbour has resonated down the centuries. The lawyer's follow up question did not address how one might achieve a whole-hearted love for God but a desire to isolate neighbourliness to Jews only.

Jesus' classic story of the man who had been robbed on his way from Jerusalem to Jericho tells us that our neighbour is the one who is prepared to put ritualistic purity aside. Priests and Levites would not wish to become ritually unclean through touching a possible dead body. The hated Samaritan was prepared to put aside national prejudice and give help at great personal cost to his Jewish enemy.

As a medical aside, it is worth noting that there is a physical cleansing effect of pouring the oil and wine into wounds. Wine has antiseptic qualities at strengths of around eleven percent alcohol. There is some evidence that olive oil aids healing. A useful property of olive oil is that it would resist the sticking of bandages to the wounds, allowing easier removal during healing.

"Go and do likewise," (v. 37) meant a complete change in the listeners' worldview. In fact, it is a change in everyone's worldview not least our own. What the Samaritan did, and what he was prepared to pay is impossible in human terms. He was prepared to write an open-ended cheque.

To love God and love our neighbour according to God's requirements are humanly impossible. "For all have sinned and fall short of the glory of God." (Romans 3:23) It means that we have to begin as disciples of Jesus and identify ourselves with the way of the cross.

Although Jesus had, "nowhere to lay His head," (Luke 9:58) there was Martha's open home. Jesus was at ease with women and treated them with far more respect than His contemporaries. Women were not usually present in "teaching seminars" and discussions. Mary was not only present, but also welcome.

Jesus' loving rebuke to Martha is advice to all of us not to be anxious about so much of our day-to-day living. We often think of Martha as only occupied with domestic concerns. John's Gospel indicates that she too was knowledgeable on spiritual matters. (John 11: 19-27) She too was aware of the "one thing needed". (v. 42) There are multitudes who seek wealth, relationships, security and go to their graves without thinking about the one thing needed, that is Jesus Himself.

Luke 11:1-36

WHAT?

1 Now it came to pass, as He was praying in a certain place, when He ceased, *that* one of His disciples said to Him, "Lord, teach us to pray, as John also taught his disciples." 2 So He said to them, "When you pray,

HoW?

say: Our Father in heaven Hallowed be Your name. Your kingdom come. Your will be done On earth as *it is* in heaven. 3 Give us day by day our daily bread. 4 And forgive us our sins, For we also forgive everyone who is indebted to us. And do not lead us into temptation, but deliver us from the evil one." 5 And He said to them, "Which of you shall have a friend, and go to him at midnight and say to him, 'Friend, lend me three loaves; 6 for a friend of mine has come to me on his journey, and I have nothing to set before him'; 7 and he will answer from within and say, 'Do not trouble

WHEN?

me; the door is now shut, and my children are with me in bed; I cannot rise and give to you'? 8 I say to you, though he will not rise and give to him because he is his friend, yet because of his persistence he will rise and give him as many as he needs. 9 So I say to you, ask, and it will be given to you; seek, and you will find; knock, and it will be opened to you. 10 For everyone who asks receives, and he who seeks finds, and to him who knocks it will be opened. 11 If a son asks for bread from any father among you, will he give him a stone? Or if *he asks* for a fish, will he give him a serpent instead of a fish? 12 Or if he asks for an egg, will he offer him a scorpion? 13 If you then, being evil, know how to give good gifts to your children, how much more will *your* heavenly Father give the Holy Spirit to those who ask Him!" 14 And He was casting out a demon, and it was mute. So it was, when the demon had gone out, that the mute spoke; and the multitudes marveled. 15 But some of them said, "He casts out demons by Beelzebub, the ruler of the demons." 16 Others, testing *Him,* sought from Him a sign from heaven. 17 But He, knowing their thoughts, said to them: "Every kingdom divided against itself is brought to desolation, and a house *divided* against a house falls. 18 If Satan also is divided against himself, how will his kingdom stand? Because you say I cast out demons by Beelzebub. 19 And if I cast out demons by Beelzebub, by whom do your sons cast *them* out? Therefore they will be your judges. 20 But if I cast out demons with the finger of God, surely the kingdom of God has come upon you. 21 When a strong man, fully armed, guards his own palace, his goods are in peace. 22 But when a stronger than he comes upon him and overcomes him, he takes from him all his armor in which he trusted, and divides his spoils. **23** He who is not with Me is against Me, and he who does not gather with Me scatters. **24** When an unclean spirit goes out of a man, he goes through dry places, seeking rest; and finding none, he says, 'I will return to my house from which I came.' **25** And when he comes, he finds *it* swept and put in order. **26** Then he goes and takes with *him* seven other spirits more wicked than himself, and they enter and dwell there; and the last *state* of that man is worse than the first." **27** And it happened, as He spoke these things, that a certain woman from the crowd raised her voice and said to Him, "Blessed *is* the womb that bore You, and *the* breasts which nursed You!" **28** But He said, "More than that, blessed *are* those who hear the word of God and keep it!" **29** And while the crowds were thickly gathered together, He began to say, "This is an evil generation. It seeks a sign, and no sign will be given to it except the sign of Jonah the prophet. **30** For as Jonah became a sign to the Ninevites, so also the Son of Man will be to this generation. **31** The queen of the South will rise up in the judgment with the men of this generation and condemn them, for she came from the ends of the earth to hear the wisdom of Solomon; and indeed a greater than Solomon *is* here. **32** The men of Nineveh will rise up in the judgment with this generation and condemn it, for they repented at the preaching of Jonah; and indeed a greater than Jonah *is* here. **33** No one, when he has lit a lamp, puts *it* in a secret place or under a basket, but on a lampstand, that those who come in may see the light. **34** The lamp of the body is the eye. Therefore, when your eye is good, your whole body also is full of light. But when *your eye* is bad, your body also *is* full of darkness. **35** Therefore take heed that the light which is in you is not darkness. **36** If then your whole body *is* full of light, having no part dark, *the* whole *body* will be full of light, as when the bright shining of a lamp gives you light."

One thing that impressed the disciples was Jesus' prayer life. It was regular and an integral part of His persona. It was natural for His disciples to ask Jesus to teach them. Prayer is a practice for those who have asked for forgiveness and accepted Jesus as their Saviour. Therefore, Jesus does not talk about posture or a mental exercise or the use of a psychological preparation, or the adoption of rhythmical swaying movements. He said, "When you pray, say." In other words, God is far more willing to listen than we are to pray, so, "Open the mouth and speak." What an example of the kindness of God that He wishes us to utter prayers.

A little before, Jesus put a child before them, (Luke 9: 47) and now Jesus invites us to use a child's address to his or her father, "Abba."

Some who have abusive fathers have found the title, "our Father" difficult. Whilst those with abusive parents should be respected and understood, it might be suggested that God should not be compared to our parents but parents should model themselves on Him.

Although Christians are forgiven people, our Lord commands us to pray regularly for forgiveness. This is a lesson in the dreadfulness of sin and God's forgiving nature. Although God is our Friend and our Father, awe and not over-familiarity is to be our attitude.

This and Matthew's larger version should be a model for our prayers. Churches with informal liturgies would be wise to include this prayer in their meetings more regularly than they do. It is our Father to whom we pray and there is a great sense of fellowship to know that this prayer is said all over the world.

Jesus then went on to expand His teaching on prayer by giving examples of the persistent friend and a son who asks.

This brings up the question of seemingly unanswered prayer.

"I prayed for my Mum to recover from her illness and she became worse." "I prayed for safety in travel and there was a terrible accident." "I prayed that my friend would get a job and she is still unemployed."

These are good prayers and we do not always know the answer. That does not mean that God does not answer prayer or that we should stop. Through all the difficulties and hardships of life we have to learn continually that "God's ways are the best ways all the time."

It is in this teaching that Jesus ended with a surprise and that was that the disciples should request God's greatest gift, the Holy Spirit. God's greatest gift is Himself and all that accompanies Him, wisdom, understanding, counsel, power, knowledge and fear of the Lord. (Isaiah 11:2) The presence of God through the Holy Spirit was present in some Old Testament saints. In the New Covenant or in other words since Jesus and the coming of the Holy Spirit on the day of Pentecost, (Acts 2) the Holy Spirit is present in all His people. The gift of the Holy Spirit means that we are saved in the world and safe in eternity.

Jesus' critics were in a dilemma. They agreed that He healed people and cast out demons and even that He performed signs. (John 3: 2) Because they could not believe that God was with Jesus, they took up the ultimate blasphemy. They said that He was empowered by the devil. This was a sign of their total and utter rejection of Jesus.

Jesus' reply showed a disarming logic. It is a quote that has been repeated by many, including Abraham Lincoln, although many are unaware that it originally came from the lips of Jesus. Matthew and Mark are slightly different in their quotation of the same incident, "Every city or house divided against itself will not stand." (Matthew 12: 25)

Jesus turned the accusation on its head and reiterated the fact that His presence and power meant that the kingdom of God had come upon them. Not only was the accusation nonsensical, it was blasphemous.

Jesus spoke wisdom which those with power and responsibility should heed. If we get rid of one source of evil, unless it is replaced by good, then the situation could become even worse.

The woman's cry from a crowd perhaps demonstrated how thinking from the Isis or ancient Artemis cult, which was present all over the ancient world, had penetrated into parts of Jewish culture. This small episode is somewhat prophetic and a warning about the extreme devotion to Mary that came upon the Christian church and is present even to this day. The word of God, the Bible, should be our sufficient guide.

The request for signs (v.29) even with all that Jesus had done and said, indicated the wrong motives behind those demands. Jesus pointed us in a graphic way towards His own resurrection. There have been many opponents of the resurrection. As was then and so is now, none can give an alternative satisfactory explanation.

Our critics believe that Christianity is dark and dangerous. Jesus here in the final verses of this passage emphasized that with Him, light has come into the world. (John 1: 9)

Luke 11:37-54

37 And as He spoke, a certain Pharisee asked Him to dine with him. So He went in and sat down to eat. **38** When the Pharisee saw *it*, he marveled that He had not first washed before dinner. **39** Then the Lord said to him, "Now you Pharisees make the outside of the cup and dish clean, but your inward part is full of greed and wickedness. **40** Foolish ones! Did not He who made the outside make the inside also? **41** But rather give alms of such things as you have; then indeed all things are clean to you. **42** But woe to you Pharisees! For you tithe mint and rue and all manner of herbs, and pass by justice and the love of God. These you ought to have done, without leaving the others undone. **43** Woe to you Pharisees! For you love the best seats in the synagogues and greetings in the marketplaces. **44** Woe to you, scribes and Pharisees, hypocrites! For you are like graves which are not seen, and the men who walk over *them* are not aware *of them.*" **45** Then one of the lawyers answered and said to Him, "Teacher, by saying these things You reproach us also." **46** And He said, "Woe to you also, lawyers! For you load men with burdens hard to bear, and you yourselves do not touch the burdens with one of your fingers. **47** Woe to you! For you build the tombs of the prophets, and your fathers killed them. **48** In fact, you bear witness that you approve the deeds of your fathers; for they indeed killed them, and you build their tombs. **49** Therefore the wisdom of God also said, 'I will send them prophets and apostles, and *some* of them they will kill and persecute,' **50** that the blood of all the prophets which was shed from the foundation of the world may be required of this generation, **51** from the blood of Abel to the blood of Zechariah who perished between the altar and the temple. Yes, I say to you, it shall be required of this generation. **52** Woe to you lawyers! For you have taken away the key of knowledge. You did not enter in yourselves, and those who were entering in you hindered." **53** And as He said these things to them, the scribes and the Pharisees began to assail *Him* vehemently, and to cross-examine Him about many things, **54** lying in wait for Him, and seeking to catch Him in something He might say, that they might accuse Him.

The visit to the Pharisee's house contains a section in the Gospel unparalleled in its content, namely the condemnation of false religion. Jesus may well have washed His hands. He was criticized that He did not perform the ceremonial washing that the traditionalists regarded as mandatory, even though it was not included in the Biblical law. They regarded that such a ritual removed contamination by sinners, reptiles, or contact with a dead body which might happen at any time during the day.

Nowhere else does Jesus express such vehement criticism as contained in these six woes. They speak of hypocrisy and evil intent cloaked by a religious exterior. (v.39) They speak of an apparent generosity but lack of care and moral compass. (v.42) They speak of the exploitation of others without any compassion towards them. They speak of a selfish desire for the trappings of status, influence and recognition in the public arena. (v.43) Jesus accused them of persecution of the true people of God and their complicity with murder of the prophets. (vv. 47-49) This horrific catalogue was aimed at those who were the leaders of religion.

The question is often asked, "Who are the Pharisees of today?"

There are those who love to take important seats, and this can be pointed at some in the old historic churches including the Roman Catholic Church. There are those who load people with burdens they can hardly carry. Some Puritans and exclusive Protestant groups have and sometimes still fit into this category. In fact the controlling "heavy shepherding" carried out by a few churches has been described as nothing else but toxic.

The truth is that this passage is a warning to subsequent generations of Christians. All of us can easily fall into the attitudes and trap of the Pharisees.

The marvellous thing is that we can get out of the trap. Nicodemus, who came to Jesus by night, was one. (John 3: 1-21)

The Apostle Paul was a Pharisee of the Pharisees. He made these comments about his past:

If anyone else thinks he may have confidence in the flesh, I more so: circumcised the eighth day, of the stock of Israel, of the tribe of Benjamin, a Hebrew of the Hebrews; concerning the law, a Pharisee; concerning zeal, persecuting the church; concerning the righteousness which is in the law, blameless. But what things were gain to me, these I have counted loss for Christ. Yet indeed I also count all things loss for the excellence of the knowledge of Christ Jesus my Lord, for whom I have suffered the loss of all things, and count them as rubbish, that I may gain Christ. (Philippians 3: 4-8)

Paul was quite specific about so much of his past thinking and attitudes. He counted them as rubbish. It took a dramatic encounter with the risen Jesus on the Damascus road to change his life. What will it take to change ours?

These words of condemnation also indicate the reason why the antipathy towards Jesus grew to the extent that led to the crucifixion.

Luke 12:1-34

1 In the meantime, when an innumerable multitude of people had gathered together, so that they trampled one another, He began to say to His disciples first *of all*, "Beware of the leaven of the Pharisees, which is hypocrisy. 2 For there is nothing covered that will not be revealed, nor hidden that will not be known. 3 Therefore whatever you have spoken in the dark will be heard in the light, and what you have spoken in the ear in inner rooms will be proclaimed on the housetops. 4 And I say to you, My friends, do not be afraid of those who kill the body, and after that have no more that they can do. 5 But I will show you whom you should fear: Fear Him who, after He has killed, has power to cast into hell; yes, I say to you, fear Him! 6 Are not five sparrows sold for two copper coins? And not one of them is forgotten before God. 7 But the very hairs of your head are all numbered. Do not fear therefore; you are of more value than many sparrows. 8 Also I say to you, whoever confesses Me before men, him the Son of Man also will confess before the angels of God. 9 But he who denies Me before men will be denied before the angels of God. 10 And anyone who speaks a word against the Son of Man, it will be forgiven him; but to him who blasphemes against the Holy Spirit, it will not be forgiven. 11 Now when they bring you to the synagogues and magistrates and authorities, do not worry about how or what you should answer, or what you should say. 12 For the Holy Spirit will teach you in that very hour what you ought to say." 13 Then one from the crowd said to Him, "Teacher, tell my brother to divide the inheritance with me." 14 But He said to him, "Man, who made Me a judge or an arbitrator over you?" 15 And He said to them, "Take heed and beware of covetousness, for one's life does not consist in the abundance of the things he possesses." 16 Then He spoke a parable to them, saying: "The ground of a certain rich man yielded plentifully. 17 And he thought within himself, saying, 'What shall I do, since I have no room to store my crops?' 18 So he said, 'I will do this: I will pull down my barns and build greater, and there I will store all my crops and my goods. 19 And I will say to my soul, "Soul, you have many goods laid up for many years; take your ease; eat, drink, *and* be merry."' 20 But God said to him, 'Fool! This night your soul will be required of you; then whose will those things be which you have provided?' 21 So *is* he who lays up treasure for himself, and is not rich toward God." 22 Then He said to His disciples, "Therefore I say to you, do not worry about your life, what you will eat; nor about the body, what you will put on. 23 Life

is more than food, and the body *is more* than clothing. **24** Consider the ravens, for they neither sow nor reap, which have neither storehouse nor barn; and God feeds them. Of how much more value are you than the birds? **25** And which of you by worrying can add one cubit to his stature? **26** If you then are not able to do *the* least, why are you anxious for the rest? **27** Consider the lilies, how they grow: they neither toil nor spin; and yet I say to you, even Solomon in all his glory was not arrayed like one of these. **28** If then God so clothes the grass, which today is in the field and tomorrow is thrown into the oven, how much more *will He clothe* you, O *you* of little faith? **29** And do not seek what you should eat or what you should drink, nor have an anxious mind. **30** For all these things the nations of the world seek after, and your Father knows that you need these things. **31** But seek the kingdom of God, and all these things shall be added to you. **32** Do not fear, little flock, for it is your Father's good pleasure to give you the kingdom. **33** Sell what you have and give alms; provide yourselves money bags which do not grow old, a treasure in the heavens that does not fail, where no thief approaches nor moth destroys. **34** For where your treasure is, there your heart will be also."

Once again Jesus warned against hypocrisy in religion. It is so dangerous that it is a road to hell. It is even more dangerous than severe physical persecution. We have genuine and legitimate concerns about the enormous persecution that has broken out during recent decades in some parts of the world. Christians have been systematically murdered and many have had to flee their homes. Jesus understood that but we should be alarmed about the effects of false religion. We who are blessed to have freedom of religion should heed Jesus' warning about surface religiosity.

He cares even to the extent that He knows the number of hairs on our heads.

Ultimately God will be the judge. The Holy Spirit will be our counsellor and comforter in the day of trial and prompt us with the right words to say.

Blasphemy against the Holy Spirit has troubled Christians for many centuries. In Matthew (Matthew 12.31-32) and Mark (Mark 3:28-29), the context is in attributing to Satan the works of Christ. It is a total, complete, utter and forever rejection of Christ and His salvation. It means that our conscience has become completely hardened to God. A wise teacher said that if you have concern about committing blasphemy against the Holy Spirit then you have not done so.

Jesus in verse 13 onwards points out the weakness of the world's foundations. We are concerned about future wealth and an adequate pension. People spend much effort, worry and energy in trying to accumulate wealth in order to "live the dream"; a time when we can live in comfort with our family around us, and not have any worries about finance and resources.

We may shrug off the day of reckoning and decision about Christ and hope to live to an active old age, right through to our nineties, and resign ourselves to one day slipping away. God said to the man in the parable who had this attitude, "You fool!"

One day all our riches will disappear. We will be accountable to God. Where is our treasure, where do we want truly to be rich? God knows we have needs and gives us much in life to enjoy, (1 Timothy 6:17) but what and where is our secure foundation?

Christians are often from needy groups in society in one way or another:

For you see your calling, brethren, that not many wise according to the flesh, not many mighty, not many noble, are called. But God has chosen the foolish things of the world to put to shame the wise, and God has chosen the weak things of the world to put to shame the things which are mighty; and the base things of the world and the things which are despised God has chosen, and the things which are not, to bring to nothing the things that are, that no flesh should glory in His presence. (1 Corinthians 1:26-29)

As a consequence, many Christians have a tendency to be anxious. Jesus used all His persuasive powers to urge us not to worry. Many a life has been stunted by worry. Day after day, Jesus puts before us the treasures of the Kingdom of Heaven:

Be anxious for nothing, but in everything by prayer and supplication, with thanksgiving, let your requests be made known to God; and the peace of God, which surpasses all understanding, will guard your hearts and minds through Christ Jesus. (Philippians 4:6-7)

The spiritual purses and treasures in Heaven will neither wear out nor rust out.

Luke 12:35-59

35 "Let your waist be girded and *your* lamps burning; **36** and you yourselves be like men who wait for their master, when he will return from the wedding, that when he comes and knocks they may open to him immediately. **37** Blessed *are* those servants whom the master, when he comes, will find watching. Assuredly, I say to you that he will gird himself and have them sit down *to eat*, and will come and serve them. **38** And if he should come in the second watch, or come in the third watch, and find *them* so, blessed are those servants. **39** But know this, that if the master of the house had known what hour the thief would come, he would have watched and not allowed his house to be broken into. **40** Therefore you also be ready, for the Son of Man is coming at an hour you do not expect." **41** Then Peter said to Him, "Lord, do You speak this parable *only* to us, or to all *people?*" **42** And the Lord said, "Who then is that faithful and wise steward, whom *his* master will make ruler over his household, to give *them their* portion of food in due season? **43** Blessed *is* that servant whom his master will find so doing when he comes. **44** Truly, I say to you that he will make him ruler over all that he has. **45** But if that servant says in his heart, 'My master is delaying his coming,' and begins to beat the male and female servants, and to eat and drink and be drunk, **46** the master of that servant will come on a day when he is not looking for *him*, and at an hour when he is not aware, and will cut him in two and appoint *him* his portion with the unbelievers. **47** And that servant who knew his master's will, and did not prepare *himself* or do according to his will, shall be beaten with many *stripes*. **48** But he who did not know, yet committed things deserving of stripes, shall be beaten with few. For everyone to whom much is given, from him much will be required; and to whom much has been committed, of him they will ask the more. **49** I came to send fire on the earth, and how I wish it were already kindled! **50** But I have a baptism to be baptized with, and how distressed I am till it is accomplished! **51** Do *you* suppose that I came to give peace on earth? I tell you, not at all, but rather division. **52** For from now on five in one house will be divided: three against two, and two against three. **53** Father will be divided against son and son against father, mother against daughter and daughter against mother, mother-in-law against her daughter-in-law and daughter-in-law against her mother-in-law." **54** Then He also said to the multitudes, "Whenever you see a cloud rising out of the west, immediately you say, 'A shower is coming'; and so it is. **55** And when *you see* the south wind blow, you say,

'There will be hot weather'; and there is. **56** Hypocrites! You can discern the face of the sky and of the earth, but how *is it* you do not discern this time? **57** Yes, and why, even of yourselves, do you not judge what is right? **58** When you go with your adversary to the magistrate, make every effort along the way to settle with him, lest he drag you to the judge, the judge deliver you to the officer, and the officer throw you into prison. **59** I tell you, you shall not depart from there till you have paid the very last mite."

In this passage Jesus gave teaching about the Second Coming. One day Jesus will return as Judge. The Bible teaches it and the Christian creeds state it. Many ignore it. There are few sermons in our churches on, "The Second Coming."

In many churches, it is an overlooked doctrine.

Firstly, Jesus said that men must be ready. Two thousand years is a long time and there may be many more years necessary to gather together all those in the future who will be given an opportunity to believe. The parable indicates that there will be those who either become lazy or will cease to believe that He will come again. Men must be ready.

Secondly, Jesus made a strong insistence on true Christianity. Drunkenness (v. 45) and abuse towards those who serve is a prevalent issue in our world. In a modern context, there are often notices in hospitals and public service buildings that say, "Do not abuse our staff." It is a persistent problem in society.

If verbal abuse comes from someone who gives profession of religion, it is a sign of an unconverted heart. We do not know the contents of a person's heart but God does. One day we will all have to give an account of our hearts' contents.

One criticism that Jews still make about Jesus is that He did not herald a grand era of peace. As has already been stated, the peace that Jesus brings is past our understanding. It is a peace that stands up in the presence of turmoil. In fact, there is and will be division. Whilst there are opponents of Christ, there will be tensions and conflicts, even in some families. Our own attitude should be one that understands, that is at peace and is aware of the times in which we live:

And let the peace of God rule in your hearts, to which also you were called in one body; and be thankful. Let the word of Christ dwell in you richly in all wisdom, teaching and admonishing one another in psalms and hymns and spiritual songs, singing with grace in your hearts to the Lord. And whatever you do in word or deed, do all in the name of the Lord Jesus, giving thanks to God the Father through Him. (Colossians 3: 15-16)

Jesus castigated the crowd because they failed to understand the times. In many ways, they had a sound understanding of the world around them.

They had all the spiritual privileges, until then, hidden from others, but they did not see them. They had the Messiah in their midst but thousands failed to recognize Him. Later Jewish authors described Jesus as "the one who had led many in Israel astray. "

They seemed to cling on to the deadening and disheartening mindset of the Pharisees and the teachers of the Law.

Today, in our materialistic outlook, thousands are oblivious of the benefits that Christianity has given to society. They leave out Jesus and hang on to the seemingly brilliant but loveless traditions of the Greco-Roman world.

We must not rely on the seemingly plausible secular attractions. Rather, we must accept the rule of a gracious Saviour before it is too late. (vv. 57-59)

Luke 13:1-21

1 There were present at that season some who told Him about the Galileans whose blood Pilate had mingled with their sacrifices. **2** And Jesus answered and said to them, "Do you suppose that these Galileans were worse sinners than all *other* Galileans, because they suffered such things? **3** I tell you, no; but unless you repent you will all likewise perish. **4** Or those eighteen on whom the tower in Siloam fell and killed them, do you think that they were worse sinners than all *other* men who dwelt in Jerusalem? **5** I tell you, no; but unless you repent you will all likewise perish." **6** He also spoke this parable: "A certain *man* had a fig tree planted in his vineyard, and he came seeking fruit on it and found none. **7** Then he said to the keeper of his vineyard, 'Look, for three years I have come seeking fruit on this fig tree and find none. Cut it down; why does it use up the ground?' **8** But he answered and said to him, 'Sir, let it alone this year also, until I dig around it and fertilize *it.* **9** And if it bears fruit, *well.* But if not, after that you can cut it down.'" **10** Now He was teaching in one of the synagogues on the Sabbath. **11** And behold, there was a woman who had a spirit of infirmity eighteen years, and was bent over and could in no way raise *herself* up. **12** But when Jesus saw her, He called *her* to *Him* and said to her, "Woman, you are loosed from your infirmity." **13** And He laid *His* hands on her, and immediately she was made straight, and glorified God. **14** But the ruler of the synagogue answered with indignation, because Jesus had healed on the Sabbath; and he said to the crowd, "There are six days on which men ought to work; therefore come and be healed on them, and not on the Sabbath day." **15** The Lord then answered him and said, "Hypocrite! Does not each one of you on the Sabbath loose his ox or donkey from the stall, and lead *it* away to water it? **16** So ought not this woman, being a daughter of Abraham, whom Satan has bound—think of it—for eighteen years, be loosed from this bond on the Sabbath?" **17** And when He said these things, all His adversaries were put to shame; and all the multitude rejoiced for all the glorious things that were done by Him. **18** Then He said, "What is the kingdom of God like? And to what shall I compare it? **19** It is like a mustard seed, which a man took and put in his garden; and it grew and became a large tree, and the birds of the air nested in its branches." **20** And again He said, "To what shall I liken the kingdom of God? **21** It is like leaven, which a woman took and hid in three measures of meal till it was all leavened."

The beginning of the Chapter mentions Pontius Pilate for the second time in Luke's Gospel. In the first verse we see something of his ruthless, cruel and insensitive character. In many ways the governorship of Judea was an impossible task amongst such a rebellious and restless population. Roman rule was stable, ordered and prosperous for those who acquiesced. For those who disagreed or displayed an independent spirit, it was quick and brutal.

tard job

hard man

The accident at Siloam demonstrated how arbitrary accidents seem to be. We never know totally what the day will bring. Whatever our status or degree of fortune, we are all together as the human race. We all need to repent and believe the Gospel.

The parable of the fig tree pointed to Israel's continued resistance to true dealings with God. It demonstrates God's extraordinary patience in the face of provocation. There will come a time when there will be a day of reckoning. If our lives are fruitful, then reward. If not, there will be eternal loss.

The next section shows, not for the first time, Jesus was in controversy over Sabbath traditions.

The woman described was tormented by an evil spirit. We do not understand all about the nature of the disability, but we do know that if for psychological or other reasons a person adopts a certain posture over a long period of time, then that posture becomes fixed. In other words, secondary physical changes take place in the body which cause the deformity to become structural and rigid. The deformity cannot be corrected by painless manipulation.

I have seen fixed postures in the upper limb, linked to psychological causes, but I have not seen a case of a psychosomatic severe flexed spine in the United Kingdom. That does not mean to say that such a rigid bent-over postures could not have been present in the ancient world.

The miracle had two parts. Firstly, Jesus freed her of the evil spirit. Secondly, she straightened up thus countering the fixed deformity.

Once again the synagogue ruler was so blinded by man-made rules that he could not see God at work in the wonder of the miracle.

166

We often think that our ways are the best and only ways. If another Christian group has success in bringing people to Christ, then instead of giving praise to God, our primary focus may be to question their ways and integrity.

Jesus observed the Sabbath according to the words of the Scriptures. The parable of the fig tree and the vineyard uses the vineyard metaphor to signify Israel. The Son of God's argument in His defence of His Sabbath observance was clear, logical and overwhelmingly patient.

The parable of the mustard seed illustrates how that great movements can arise from the smallest of beginnings. Not only that, others can benefit from the outcome.

Jesus later spoke about another seed shortly before the crucifixion:

But Jesus answered them, saying, "The hour has come that the Son of Man should be glorified. Most assuredly, I say to you, unless a grain of wheat falls into the ground and dies, it remains alone; but if it dies, it produces much grain. He who loves his life will lose it, and he who hates his life in this world will keep it for eternal life........ And I, if I am lifted up from the earth, will draw all peoples to Myself." This He said, signifying by what death He would die. (John 12: 23-33)

Thousands upon thousands were crucified during the Roman era. One crucifixion, that of Jesus, brings salvation to all who come to Him. What started from the most apparently disastrous beginning has become a worldwide movement.

The next illustration shows how a little yeast can affect the whole loaf of bread. Similarly a small group of Christians can have impressions on a whole society.

In the United Kingdom many of our laws have been framed around the Ten Commandments and the Judeo-Christian tradition, although recent developments have tended to move away from that ethos. Many in the United Kingdom have given themselves some form of Christian label although few would say that they were committed to Christ. Like the yeast in the loaf, the number of Christians is comparatively small. Let us be faithful and resolved each day to continue in a wonderful discipleship, in the knowledge that God can do great things with His small number of followers.

167

Luke 13:22-35

22 And He went through the cities and villages, teaching, and journeying toward Jerusalem. **23** Then one said to Him, "Lord, are there few who are saved?" And He said to them, **24** "Strive to enter through the narrow gate, for many, I say to you, will seek to enter and will not be able. **25** When once the Master of the house has risen up and shut the door, and you begin to stand outside and knock at the door, saying, 'Lord, Lord, open for us,' and He will answer and say to you, 'I do not know you, where you are from,' **26** then you will begin to say, 'We ate and drank in Your presence, and You taught in our streets.' **27** But He will say, 'I tell you I do not know you, where you are from. Depart from Me, all you workers of iniquity.' **28** There will be weeping and gnashing of teeth, when you see Abraham and Isaac and Jacob and all the prophets in the kingdom of God, and yourselves thrust out. **29** They will come from the east and the west, from the north and the south, and sit down in the kingdom of God. **30** And indeed there are last who will be first, and there are first who will be last." **31** On that very day some Pharisees came, saying to Him, "Get out and depart from here, for Herod wants to kill You." **32** And He said to them, "Go, tell that fox, 'Behold, I cast out demons and perform cures today and tomorrow, and the third *day* I shall be perfected.' **33** Nevertheless I must journey today, tomorrow, and the *day* following; for it cannot be that a prophet should perish outside of Jerusalem. **34** O Jerusalem, Jerusalem, the one who kills the prophets and stones those who are sent to her! How often I wanted to gather your children together, as a hen *gathers* her brood under *her* wings, but you were not willing! **35** See! Your house is left to you desolate; and assuredly, I say to you, you shall not see Me until *the time* comes when you say, 'Blessed is He who comes in the name of the Lord!' "

At this point, Luke reminds us that Jesus was on the way to Jerusalem. We must be clear that although Jesus was killed by violent men, He knew what was going to happen and He went to Jerusalem voluntarily. He was "obedient to the point of death, even the death on the cross". (Philippians 2: 8)

The question, "Are there few who are saved?" (v. 23) is amongst the most important questions one can ask. It is in the same vein as, "How can I be saved?"

Jesus' reply that we should strive to enter through the narrow gate (v.24), should sink into every reader's heart. Jesus was clear, direct, and shocking. It puts an end to the freewheeling, easy-riding religion that many think is just fine. It puts an end to the validity of an outward show of religiosity coupled with an inward unbelief.

It was Jesus who said, "You must be born again" and "One thing is needed" and "The kingdom of God is at hand" and "Repent, and believe the Gospel."

He was the most severe in His condemnation of hypocritical religion, and yet the most compassionate to those who knew their need of God. The narrow gate stands before all who hear the Gospel. "Should I bother, should I strive?"

Salvation is all of God. He provides; He calls according to His will; He draws, and He completes. God is sovereign in His choice, and yet we are urged to strive. We still have a responsibility to strive to enter the narrow gate. These are warnings as well as paradoxes. Let us not rest until we have given a satisfactory answer to the question put before us.

As well as being alarming, Jesus' words are comforting, since there will be those who come from all over the world to "sit down in the kingdom of God". The book of Revelation refers to a vast horde of believers that no man can number. (Revelation 7:9)

Billions will have inhabited the Earth. In comparison with that, we are confronted with the solemn words that the gate is still narrow and comparatively few will find it.

The final five verses show the difference between the kingdoms of this world and the kingdom of Jesus which is not of this world. The first type of ruler has to maintain power by the sword. Herod had already executed John the Baptist because of John's criticism of the king's adultery. He was ruthless like his father, Herod the Great, who killed members of his own family. In Britain, five hundred years ago, people were executed if they were critical of the king's divorce. In other countries even today, opponents of regimes are known to disappear. Fortunately the tender flower of democracy means that people are stood down rather than suffer assassination.

We must remember that, with notable exceptions, people in power rarely are sincere in their profession of faith. Political leaders tend to praise religion and use the church if it suits their own ends.

Jesus wept over Jerusalem and wants to gather people into His kingdom. It is a kingdom of love and persuasion. However, whatever despots and mockers will say and do, He is still the judge of all the world. His prophecies will all come to pass and His word never fails. God wins in the end.

We do not know why the Pharisees warned Jesus. It may be because they wanted Jesus to move to another jurisdiction. Since Jesus began His ministry, some of the Nazareth synagogue had wanted to kill Him, (Luke 4:29) some Pharisees had been plotting to get rid of Jesus, (Luke 6:11) and another, Herod now wanted to kill Him. (v.31) Jesus knew all this and referred to Herod as "that fox", an animal known for its cunning.

Lastly, it needs to be pointed out that except on rare occasions such as this one, generally speaking, we should refer to rulers with a deal of respect:

Therefore submit yourselves to every ordinance of man for the Lord's sake, whether to the king as supreme, or to governors, as to those who are sent by him for the punishment of evildoers and for the praise of those who do good. For this is the will of God, that by doing good you may put to silence the ignorance of foolish men – as free, yet not using liberty as a cloak for vice, but as bondservants of God. Honour all people. Love the brotherhood. Fear God. Honour the king. (1 Peter 2:13-17)

It requires great discernment and patience to achieve a right balance. Many Christians have agonized over this issue of respect for those in authority and denunciation of injustices. There is much need for prayer and wisdom.

Luke 14:1-11

1 Now it happened, as He went into the house of one of the rulers of the Pharisees to eat bread on the Sabbath, that they watched Him closely. **2** And behold, there was a certain man before Him who had dropsy. **3** And Jesus, answering, spoke to the lawyers and Pharisees, saying, "Is it lawful to heal on the Sabbath?" **4** But they kept silent. And He took *him* and healed him, and let him go. **5** Then He answered them, saying, "Which of you, having a donkey or an ox that has fallen into a pit, will not immediately pull him out on the Sabbath day?" **6** And they could not answer Him regarding these things. **7** So He told a parable to those who were invited, when He noted how they chose the best places, saying to them: **8** "When you are invited by anyone to a wedding feast, do not sit down in the best place, lest one more honorable than you be invited by him; **9** and he who invited you and him come and say to you, 'Give place to this man,' and then you begin with shame to take the lowest place. **10** But when you are invited, go and sit down in the lowest place, so that when he who invited you comes he may say to you, 'Friend, go up higher.' Then you will have glory in the presence of those who sit at the table with you. **11** For whoever exalts himself will be humbled, and he who humbles himself will be exalted."

In this Chapter, Jesus, as a teaching Rabbi, was invited to dine with a Pharisee and was surrounded by His critics. It is a situation which would be unnerving and uncomfortable for most of us, but Jesus conducted Himself with patience, measured clarity and dignity.

Once again, Jesus is confronted by Sabbath traditional observance. The teachers thought it was not lawful to heal on the Sabbath, but had no reason or quote to back up their view. It seems to have been "a given". They said nothing because all they had were their traditions and prejudices.

It is a little like the belief in Darwinian evolution. When a reasoned objection is put forward, it is automatically rejected without discussion since the standard view is that Darwinian evolution must have taken place. All criticisms must therefore be wrong.

Dropsy is a word which is only used once in the New Testament and was a medical term of those days. It denoted fluid retention which would have caused swelling, particularly in the lower limbs. The causes of fluid retention or oedema are numerous and include kidney and liver disease. Chronic heart failure can also be responsible for dependent oedema. Whatever the cause, he received healing. We know nothing about the man, or his faith or subsequent life. He was one of the many healed by Jesus during His earthly ministry.

To the religious leaders, instead of a cause for praise, the man became a source of contention. Jesus answered His detractors with unassailable logic. Let us work and pray for suitable explanations for the faith that is within us. (1 Peter 3: 15)

Jesus went on to illustrate true Christian humility. The Christian is not a doormat, but only the Christian has an understanding of God's power and holiness, and our need for grace and forgiveness. The Christian is not to be in the business of self-glory, self-promotion and self-aggrandizement. The Christian is to be prepared to be placed in a low position and identify with those with little privilege. Paul helps us in his description of love:

Love suffers long and is kind; love does not envy; love does not parade itself, is not puffed up; does not behave rudely, does not seek its own, is not provoked, thinks no evil; does not rejoice in iniquity, but rejoices in the truth; bears all things, believes all things, hopes all things, endures all things. (1 Corinthians 13: 4-7)

Jesus showed us an example when He took on the role of a servant during the "Last Supper". There, He took a towel and basin, stooped and washed the disciples' feet. (John 13: 3-11) We should be proud of our Saviour but not because of any position we might be given. Many of us have lessons to learn in the area of pride, false humility, and true humility.

Wise is the saying of the proverb:

Pride goes before destruction, And a haughty spirit before a fall. Better to be of a humble spirit with the lowly, Than to divide the spoil with the proud. (Proverbs 16: 18-19)

Anaemic

old # leg
Bd'. mass
protein acunes
of h lebitie

Luke 14:12-35

12 Then He also said to him who invited Him, "When you give a dinner or a supper, do not ask your friends, your brothers, your relatives, nor rich neighbors, lest they also invite you back, and you be repaid. **13** But when you give a feast, invite *the* poor, *the* maimed, *the* lame, *the* blind. **14** And you will be blessed, because they cannot repay you; for you shall be repaid at the resurrection of the just." **15** Now when one of those who sat at the table with Him heard these things, he said to Him, "Blessed *is* he who shall eat bread in the kingdom of God!" **16** Then He said to him, "A certain man gave a great supper and invited many, **17** and sent his servant at supper time to say to those who were invited, 'Come, for all things are now ready.' **18** But they all with one *accord* began to make excuses. The first said to him, 'I have bought a piece of ground, and I must go and see it. I ask you to have me excused.' **19** And another said, 'I have bought five yoke of oxen, and I am going to test them. I ask you to have me excused.' **20** Still another said, 'I have married a wife, and therefore I cannot come.' **21** So that servant came and reported these things to his master. Then the master of the house, being angry, said to his servant, 'Go out quickly into the streets and lanes of the city, and bring in here *the* poor and *the* maimed and *the* lame and *the* blind.' **22** And the servant said, 'Master, it is done as you commanded, and still there is room.' **23** Then the master said to the servant, 'Go out into the highways and hedges, and compel *them* to come in, that my house may be filled. **24** For I say to you that none of those men who were invited shall taste my supper.'" **25** Now great multitudes went with Him. And He turned and said to them, **26** "If anyone comes to Me and does not hate his father and mother, wife and children, brothers and sisters, yes, and his own life also, he cannot be My disciple. **27** And whoever does not bear his cross and come after Me cannot be My disciple. **28** For which of you, intending to build a tower, does not sit down first and count the cost, whether he has *enough* to finish *it*— **29** lest, after he has laid the foundation, and is not able to finish, all who see *it* begin to mock him, **30** saying, 'This man began to build and was not able to finish'? **31** Or what king, going to make war against another king, does not sit down first and consider whether he is able with ten thousand to meet him who comes against him with twenty thousand? **32** Or else, while the other is still a great way off, he sends a delegation and asks conditions of peace. **33** So likewise, whoever of you does not forsake all that he has cannot be

My disciple. **34** Salt *is* good; but if the salt has lost its flavor, how shall it be seasoned? **35** It is neither fit for the land nor for the dunghill, *but* men throw it out. He who has ears to hear, let him hear!"

Many invite friends and neighbours to meals and other social occasions and it is easy to feel snubbed when the gift is not returned. We come to expect it. Jesus indicated that not only should we not expect it, but that we should invite those from time to time who are not in a position to invite us back. Faithful churches contain a vast social mix. There are often many whom we would not meet socially. There are different temperaments and backgrounds. In a godly fellowship, those who have the facility to give hospitality will honour God if they do so ungrudgingly and wholeheartedly.

The parable of the banquet gives us an illustration of those who refuse Jesus' gracious, kind invitation to follow Him. Those who have ability and means will be tempted to make their activities of wealth-creation, career and relationships a priority. It is a sad and true observation that people state that they are too busy to have time for God or Sunday worship. One day, at the last judgment, they will realize that they had all the time that was required to respond to the offer of salvation, as well as earning a living and forming stable families. There will be many regrets on that day.

The ones who did come to the banquet were those at the bottom of the social, economic and physical pile. The physically-challenged were not allowed into the temple courts of Israel, but Jesus offered them the greatest of welcomes to the heavenly banquet of the kingdom of God.

Although Jesus' life was under pressure from various authorities, He still attracted large crowds. Their motives were not all clear, but a better life from selfish perspectives would have been high on many agendas.

Jesus confronts us with a number of difficult issues. Respect and honour for parents was part of the Ten Commandments. (Exodus 20: 12) Jesus did not contradict the commandment. However, if we had to choose between Jesus and injunctions from family members, then Jesus comes first. The word "hate" that Jesus used is a Hebrew literary means of emphasis or hyperbole. Being a Christian does not negate our responsibilities to our parents and family, but on the contrary helps us increase our sense of responsibility and care.

But if anyone does not provide for his own, and especially for those of his household, he has denied the faith and is worse than an unbeliever. (1 Timothy 5:8)

The parables of the tower and the king and his army are an indication that being a Christian is not like being a signed-up member of an occasional club but rather a complete commitment. So many begin on that path but are unable to continue because they have not counted the cost. Having worked with Joseph as a carpenter, Jesus would have known about all the necessary means to complete a building project.

The parable of the king who needs to plan carefully before waging war is not a praise of armed conflict but a warning that being a Christian may be a life and death struggle. This became clear later under Roman rule and has been true in many parts of the world to this day. It has been estimated that there have been more Christian martyrs since World War II than in the rest of Christian history.

Those who give a mere nominal allegiance to Christ are like salt without its properties of taste and preservation.

Luke 15:1-32

1 Then all the tax collectors and the sinners drew near to Him to hear Him. 2 And the Pharisees and scribes complained, saying, "This Man receives sinners and eats with them." 3 So He spoke this parable to them, saying: 4 "What man of you, having a hundred sheep, if he loses one of them, does not leave the ninety-nine in the wilderness, and go after the one which is lost until he finds it? 5 And when he has found *it*, he lays *it* on his shoulders, rejoicing. 6 And when he comes home, he calls together *his* friends and neighbors, saying to them, 'Rejoice with me, for I have found my sheep which was lost!' 7 I say to you that likewise there will be more joy in heaven over one sinner who repents than over ninety-nine just persons who need no repentance. 8 Or what woman, having ten silver coins, if she loses one coin, does not light a lamp, sweep the house, and search carefully until she finds *it*? 9 And when she has found *it*, she calls *her* friends and neighbors together, saying, 'Rejoice with me, for I have found the piece which I lost!' 10 Likewise, I say to you, there is joy in the presence of the angels of God over one sinner who repents." 11 Then He said: "A certain man had two sons. 12 And the younger of them said to *his* father, 'Father, give me the portion of goods that falls *to me*.' So he divided to them *his* livelihood. 13 And not many days after, the younger son gathered all together, journeyed to a far country, and there wasted his possessions with prodigal living. 14 But when he had spent all, there arose a severe famine in that land, and he began to be in want. 15 Then he went and joined himself to a citizen of that country, and he sent him into his fields to feed swine. 16 And he would gladly have filled his stomach with the pods that the swine ate, and no one gave him *anything.* 17 But when he came to himself, he said, 'How many of my father's hired servants have bread enough and to spare, and I perish with hunger! 18 I will arise and go to my father, and will say to him, "Father, I have sinned against heaven and before you, 19 and I am no longer worthy to be called your son. Make me like one of your hired servants."' 20 And he arose and came to his father. But when he was still a great way off, his father saw him and had compassion, and ran and fell on his neck and kissed him. 21 And the son said to him, 'Father, I have sinned against heaven and in your sight, and am no longer worthy to be called your son.' 22 But the father said to his servants, 'Bring out the best robe and put *it* on him, and put a ring on his hand and sandals on *his* feet. 23 And bring the fatted calf here and kill

it, and let us eat and be merry; **24** for this my son was dead and is alive again; he was lost and is found.' And they began to be merry. **25** Now his older son was in the field. And as he came and drew near to the house, he heard music and dancing. **26** So he called one of the servants and asked what these things meant. **27** And he said to him, 'Your brother has come, and because he has received him safe and sound, your father has killed the fatted calf.' **28** But he was angry and would not go in. Therefore his father came out and pleaded with him. **29** So he answered and said to *his* father, 'Lo, these many years I have been serving you; I never transgressed your commandment at any time; and yet you never gave me a young goat, that I might make merry with my friends. **30** But as soon as this son of yours came, who has devoured your livelihood with harlots, you killed the fatted calf for him.' **31** And he said to him, 'Son, you are always with me, and all that I have is yours. **32** It was right that we should make merry and be glad, for your brother was dead and is alive again, and was lost and is found."

"This Man welcomes sinners and eats with them." (v. 2) Since those words were first uttered, the insult has become a crowning glory. No matter how bad or good we have been, we are all sinners and all are welcomed by the Saviour. In a way we find difficult to understand, Jesus' sacrificial death on the cross has made the welcome possible. One of the main problems is that most believe that we can achieve a satisfactory standard by our own ends and therefore are not in need of forgiveness. The mindset of the Pharisees has lived on down the centuries in many and various guises.

The parables of the lost sheep and the lost coin are illustrations of the ungrudging completeness of God's welcome.

Jesus is pictured as being prepared to leave behind those who appear safe but are self-righteous and actively pursuing the lost sheep. It is a wonderful picture of the grace of God that He is totally, lovingly interested in each one of us as an individual.

Our reception into God's kingdom is not graded or subtly secret. It is a welcome with rejoicing.

The second parable is an example of the upheaval on God's part to search out the "not yet believer". The coin was normally worn with a series of others on the woman's headscarf. It was part of the marriage gift and therefore a most precious object. This is one parable where a woman is the key participant.

The lost one who finds repentance is not only welcomed with rejoicing but all the angels in Heaven celebrate. It is overwhelming and beyond imagination.

The parable of "the prodigal son" is many-layered and profound in its understanding of so many human and family situations. Every generation has its number of both wayward and the seemingly loyal but grudging sons.

The son who wanted his inheritance immediately expressed an underlying wish to see his father dead. He knew best and the attractions of the glitzy world of endless partying and pleasure were too much for him to resist. In every decade there are hordes who have gone to and remained in the lifestyle of that far-off, self-indulgent country. Today, with our phones and computers, we do not have to travel at all. Sexual bullying and sexting have become prevalent in every school. Nevertheless, Britons still travel to holiday in particular resorts to emulate the activities of the first son. There is nothing new.

It took a rock-bottom experience to make the young man come to his senses. He became an exploited labourer who worked amongst animals that Jews would have considered to be unclean. It was at that point that the home and values of his father became what he really wanted. And so, he set off for home believing that his father would be loving and forgiving even if he was to become a servant on the farm.

The father who waited longingly for his son was prepared to run towards him, an activity a gentleman would not normally have done. He threw his arms around his ceremonially and literally unclean son and restored the repentant young man to his former position.

The elder son resented the celebration party. He claimed to have been totally loyal and obedient. Nevertheless, in a different way to his brother, he too did not appreciate the nature of his father's love. His attitude was just like the Pharisees and religious leaders of the day.

Are we prepared to be in the position of God's plan and place for us? Are we like the younger son who learnt the hard way about becoming and being a Christian, or are we harbouring attitudes of resentment and self-righteousness like the elder son?

Earlier, Jesus talked about the way of the cross. (Luke 14: 27) It is a way we must follow, but there is also a joy before us:

Therefore we also, since we are surrounded by so great a cloud of witnesses, let us lay aside every weight, and the sin which so easily ensnares us, and let us run with endurance the race that is set before us, looking unto Jesus, the author and finisher of our faith, who for the joy that was set before Him endured the cross, despising the shame, and has sat down at the right hand of the throne of God. (Hebrews 12:1-2)

Luke 16:1-18

1 He also said to His disciples: "There was a certain rich man who had a steward, and an accusation was brought to him that this man was wasting his goods. 2 So he called him and said to him, 'What is this I hear about you? Give an account of your stewardship, for you can no longer be steward.' 3 Then the steward said within himself, 'What shall I do? For my master is taking the stewardship away from me. I cannot dig; I am ashamed to beg. 4 I have resolved what to do, that when I am put out of the stewardship, they may receive me into their houses.' 5 So he called every one of his master's debtors to *him*, and said to the first, 'How much do you owe my master?' 6 And he said, 'A hundred measures of oil.' So he said to him, 'Take your bill, and sit down quickly and write fifty.' 7 Then he said to another, 'And how much do you owe?' So he said, 'A hundred measures of wheat.' And he said to him, 'Take your bill, and write eighty.' 8 So the master commended the unjust steward because he had dealt shrewdly. For the sons of this world are more shrewd in their generation than the sons of light. 9 And I say to you, make friends for yourselves by unrighteous mammon, that when you fail, they may receive you into an everlasting home. 10 He who *is* faithful in *what is* least is faithful also in much; and he who is unjust in *what is* least is unjust also in much. 11 Therefore if you have not been faithful in the unrighteous mammon, who will commit to your trust the true *riches?* 12 And if you have not been faithful in what is another man's, who will give you what is your own? 13 No servant can serve two masters; for either he will hate the one and love the other, or else he will be loyal to the one and despise the other. You cannot serve God and mammon." 14 Now the Pharisees, who were lovers of money, also heard all these things, and they derided Him. 15 And He said to them, "You are those who justify yourselves before men, but God knows your hearts. For what is highly esteemed among men is an abomination in the sight of God. 16 The law and the prophets *were* until John. Since that time the kingdom of God has been preached, and everyone is pressing into it. 17 And it is easier for heaven and earth to pass away than for one tittle of the law to fail. 18 Whoever divorces his wife and marries another commits adultery; and whoever marries her who is divorced from *her* husband commits adultery."

How shrewd are we? The world is full of people who manipulate, and are admired, even for their shady deals. We call them chancers, wideboys, opportunists, spivs or even entrepreneurs. The parable is not easy to understand and both the ruler and the steward were flawed men of the world. The ruler praised the unjust steward because unexpectedly, he had been outwitted.

The parable does not wish us to emulate their dishonesty, but Christians need to be alert that others are like this and be aware of all that goes on. We must avoid being pulled into that mode of thinking.

Opponents of Christianity have used this parable to malign Christ's integrity. It has to be admitted that there are difficulties over this passage, but such an accusation betrays a superficial, ill-considered reading of these verses, and an ignorance of the other Gospel passages.

Jesus urged us to be more wise than the world. Whatever resources we have, they can be used to help people become Christians. Jesus encouraged us to employ friendship and use our minds to invest in the kingdom of God.

All who are well-off are easy prey to an acquisitive mindset, and tend to develop an increasing desire for more. The Pharisees saw their wealth as a sign of God's favour. Jesus gave us a stark warning which all Christians should take to heart. We cannot serve two masters. We cannot serve both God and money.

A right balance in our attitude to money is essential. Jesus talked more about money than any one else in the Bible. He understood money's power to corrupt the human mind. He also knew that sound financial management and probity is crucial in any enterprise. (Luke 14:28) Anyone competent and sound in the areas of administration is usually trustworthy over deeper spiritual duties. Examples of this were the first appointed deacons who administered the distribution to widows. The deacons included Philip who was later known as the Evangelist, (Acts 21:8) and Stephen who became a great communicator of the Gospel. (Acts 6:8)

A Christian accountant needs to be full of the Holy Spirit. (Acts 6:3) Many Christian organizations have suffered because of poor attention to financial matters.

Jesus exposed the acquisitive nature of His detractors. He knew that the surface respectability hid a darker side. The true Gospel, in spite of all the obstacles put up by false religionists, is attractive to every type of person. It has become a worldwide movement in a vast number of different cultures.

Christ's teaching on divorce has exercised the minds of many faithful teachers. We cannot get the whole picture here, but it appears that many first century religious leaders treated their wives like possessions. Because of their wealth, they were able to divorce and remarry over trivial reasons. Throughout history, too many men have treated their wives without sympathy, consideration or any sense of partnership. They have been keen to emphasize their wives' obedience, but not their own requirement to love their wives as their own bodies:

Husbands, love your wives, just as Christ also loved the church and gave Himself for her, that He might sanctify and cleanse her with the washing of water by the word, that He might present her to Himself a glorious church, not having spot or wrinkle or any such thing, but that she should be holy and without blemish. So husbands ought to love their own wives as their own bodies; he who loves his wife loves himself. For no one ever hated his own flesh, but nourishes and cherishes it, just as the Lord does the church. (Ephesians 5: 25-29)

Luke 16:19-31

19 "There was a certain rich man who was clothed in purple and fine linen and fared sumptuously every day. **20** But there was a certain beggar named Lazarus, full of sores, who was laid at his gate, **21** desiring to be fed with the crumbs which fell from the rich man's table. Moreover the dogs came and licked his sores. **22** So it was that the beggar died, and was carried by the angels to Abraham's bosom. The rich man also died and was buried. **23** And being in torments in Hades, he lifted up his eyes and saw Abraham afar off, and Lazarus in his bosom. **24** Then he cried and said, 'Father Abraham, have mercy on me, and send Lazarus that he may dip the tip of his finger in water and cool my tongue; for I am tormented in this flame.' **25** But Abraham said, 'Son, remember that in your lifetime you received your good things, and likewise Lazarus evil things; but now he is comforted and you are tormented. **26** And besides all this, between us and you there is a great gulf fixed, so that those who want to pass from here to you cannot, nor can those from there pass to us.' **27** Then he said, 'I beg you therefore, father, that you would send him to my father's house, **28** for I have five brothers, that he may testify to them, lest they also come to this place of torment.' **29** Abraham said to him, 'They have Moses and the prophets; let them hear them.' **30** And he said, 'No, father Abraham; but if one goes to them from the dead, they will repent.' **31** But he said to him, 'If they do not hear Moses and the prophets, neither will they be persuaded though one rise from the dead.'"

This parable contains vivid and heart rending imagery.

Firstly, there is the inescapable fact that death is the great leveller. Modern medicine and technology has increased life-expectancy in most parts of the world. However, old or young, rich or poor, in pain or quietly, we all pass along the valley of the shadow of death. Sooner or later, fair or unfair, death is inevitable.

Secondly, we note that Jesus asserted that there is life after death and that there is a clear divine judgment. We do not move into a state of mere oblivion as many modern thinkers suppose. We are either with Christ or we are far away in a sense of torment. There is no halfway house.

Thirdly, the rich man had all of what are considered to be the good things in life. He had money, popularity, status, and a marvellous home. He lived the dream. His self-obsession gave him little time to think about his relationship with God since in everything he was self satisfied. He lived without any sideways glance towards the needs of others.

He gave no thought to Lazarus who sat at his gate with physical ailments, licked by dogs, and no other means of support. The beggar did not blame or curse God or lose faith in God. He was in a similar condition to that of Job, the Old Testament man of God.

Although they were poles apart on earth, the status of the two men reversed in the afterlife.

Then Jesus said two shocking things. The rich man who enjoyed life to the full found himself in outer darkness. That status could have been altered during his own lifetime if he had come to God in repentance. Zacchaeus did just that – as we will read later in the Gospel. Sadly, after death, it was too late.

The rich man's desire to send warnings to his brothers would not work. They would not believe even if Jesus rose from the dead. (v.31)

In spite of all the evidence in favour of Jesus' resurrection, (v. 31) opponents of Christianity have and always will scoff at the notion. Some are so comfortable in this life that they will never see their need of God.

This parable disturbs the comfortable and asks searching questions.

Am I forgiven and in a right relationship with God? Do I consider those in need, in or outside the next house, street, town or nation?

We can have a right relationship with God, which will enable us to show love for others. However, in another sense, we can never do enough to succeed in alleviating all the poverty and needs of others. The task is overwhelming, but God has something for each one of us to do.

Luke 17:1-19

1 Then He said to the disciples, "It is impossible that no offenses should come, but woe *to him* through whom they do come! **2** It would be better for him if a millstone were hung around his neck, and he were thrown into the sea, than that he should offend one of these little ones. **3** Take heed to yourselves. If your brother sins against you, rebuke him; and if he repents, forgive him. **4** And if he sins against you seven times in a day, and seven times in a day returns to you, saying, 'I repent,' you shall forgive him." **5** And the apostles said to the Lord, "Increase our faith." **6** So the Lord said, "If you have faith as a mustard seed, you can say to this mulberry tree, 'Be pulled up by the roots and be planted in the sea,' and it would obey you. **7** And which of you, having a servant plowing or tending sheep, will say to him when he has come in from the field, 'Come at once and sit down to eat'? **8** But will he not rather say to him, 'Prepare something for my supper, and gird yourself and serve me till I have eaten and drunk, and afterward you will eat and drink'? **9** Does he thank that servant because he did the things that were commanded him? I think not. **10** So likewise you, when you have done all those things which you are commanded, say, 'We are unprofitable servants. We have done what was our duty to do.'" **11** Now it happened as He went to Jerusalem that He passed through the midst of Samaria and Galilee. **12** Then as He entered a certain village, there met Him ten men who were lepers, who stood afar off. **13** And they lifted up *their* voices and said, "Jesus, Master, have mercy on us!" **14** So when He saw *them,* He said to them, "Go, show yourselves to the priests." And so it was that as they went, they were cleansed. **15** And one of them, when he saw that he was healed, returned, and with a loud voice glorified God, **16** and fell down on *his* face at His feet, giving Him thanks. And he was a Samaritan. **17** So Jesus answered and said, "Were there not ten cleansed? But where *are* the nine? **18** Were there not any found who returned to give glory to God except this foreigner?" **19** And He said to him, "Arise, go your way. Your faith has made you well."

This group of sayings following on from the previous Chapter helps us enlarge our understanding of the Christian experience. There are always going to be mistakes and we will from time to time make unguarded remarks that bring stains on our reputation and that of the Gospel. We must be on our guard to ensure that the only offence is that of the cross. Jesus was particularly concerned that our example does not offend youngsters or those who are weak in the faith. I am sure that some have been "taken out" of ministry by one means or another because of scandal or false teaching. It is not for us to persecute a false teacher. Jesus put the situation in such stark terms, (v.2) in order to emphasize the danger that they present.

One offence that Jesus pointed out is that of an unforgiving heart. Revenge and resentment is not part of the Christian's toolbox. Forgiveness speaks volumes about the loving nature of our God. Often, what people see is more important than what people hear.

The apostles had been presented with such astonishing teaching that they could only say, "Increase our faith." In spite of all they had seen from the miracles of our Lord, they, just like us, felt a sense of faith-insecurity. Jesus' reply indicated how that we can accomplish great things for God even from small beginnings like those of a mustard seed. Who would have thought that these ordinary Christian apostles would be instrumental in spreading the Gospel throughout the Roman Empire within a generation or so?

We all need to remind ourselves that none of us deserve Heaven or achieve it on merit. (vv. 7-10) We are not entitled to rewards. They are things which God gives according to His choice and grace alone. We are indeed "unprofitable servants".

Chapter 5 includes an incident where Jesus touched and healed a leper. On this occasion here there are ten of them, and because of their unclean status, they stood away and at a distance. They would have heard about Jesus' ministry and it could be just possible that He could do something for them. It was yet another interruption which prompted a demonstration of overwhelming power and love, not only to individuals but also to a group.

The story also demonstrates our tendency to use Jesus and treat Him with the perspective of a corrupt heart. His job is to do stuff for us! That is why those who believe that they are comfortable in this world more often than not have little time for Jesus.

It is a sad reflection on humanity that only one of them praised God, offered allegiance to Jesus as one would to a king and thanked Him. No wonder Jesus often urged people to be quiet about what He had done for them. Luke, once again, demonstrated how that Jesus was there for everyone including foreigners. He did not treat them with suspicion and aloofness as is customary with humanity in general.

Earlier, the apostles had asked for increased faith. At the end of this section, (v.19) our Saviour commended the faith of a poor, outcast, leper foreigner, the one out of the ten that had been healed.

Luke 17:20-37

20 Now when He was asked by the Pharisees when the kingdom of God would come, He answered them and said, "The kingdom of God does not come with observation; **21** nor will they say, 'See here!' or 'See there!' For indeed, the kingdom of God is within you." **22** Then He said to the disciples, "The days will come when you will desire to see one of the days of the Son of Man, and you will not see *it*. **23** And they will say to you, 'Look here!' or 'Look there!' Do not go after *them* or follow *them*. **24** For as the lightning that flashes out of one *part* under heaven shines to the other *part* under heaven, so also the Son of Man will be in His day. **25** But first He must suffer many things and be rejected by this generation. **26** And as it was in the days of Noah, so it will be also in the days of the Son of Man: **27** They ate, they drank, they married wives, they were given in marriage, until the day that Noah entered the ark, and the flood came and destroyed them all. **28** Likewise as it was also in the days of Lot: They ate, they drank, they bought, they sold, they planted, they built; **29** but on the day that Lot went out of Sodom it rained fire and brimstone from heaven and destroyed *them* all. **30** Even so will it be in the day when the Son of Man is revealed. **31** "In that day, he who is on the housetop, and his goods *are* in the house, let him not come down to take them away. And likewise the one who is in the field, let him not turn back. **32** Remember Lot's wife. **33** Whoever seeks to save his life will lose it, and whoever loses his life will preserve it. **34** I tell you, in that night there will be two *men* in one bed: the one will be taken and the other will be left. **35** Two *women* will be grinding together: the one will be taken and the other left. **36** Two *men* will be in the field: the one will be taken and the other left." **37** And they answered and said to Him, "Where, Lord?" So He said to them, "Wherever the body is, there the eagles will be gathered together."

The Pharisees with all their suspicions of Jesus were wondering if anything else was going to develop in Jesus' ministry. Like so many of their contemporaries, and indeed Muslims today, they equated the Kingdom of God with a type of religious political state under a system of what they believed to be divine laws. Jesus emphasized that you cannot walk into a town or declare an edict and say, "Here it is!" God's kingdom is about your heart, your spiritual state, your conscience, your allegiance and your motivation. It is about our own surrender to Jesus Himself.

After speaking to the Pharisees, Jesus switched His attention to the disciples who still hankered after a restored Israel. They did so even up to the time of Jesus' ascension. (Acts 1: 6)

However, as in many things of Jesus, there is more than one level in His teaching. He often spoke simultaneously about the present, future and end times. In the future, believers in their trials and under persecution will long for Christ's coming. There will be a new kingdom and that will be at His second coming. There will be nothing secret or hidden about it. It will be obvious to all and come at a time men least expect.

In the meantime, we are not to go after personalities who claim to have special knowledge about the timing of the event. It will be sudden and will involve a great divide. Some will be taken and others left.

Commentators have differed in their interpretations of verses 34-36. Some have thought that the taken ones are those taken to be with Christ at "The Rapture". Others say that the taken ones are those who are taken to destruction. Whatever is correct, it is clear that even amongst family, friends and work colleagues, there is a great division. That division depends on our position with regards to Jesus. It will be no use pleading association or friendship with a believer or having worked in a certain office or sang in a church related choir. Are we with Him or against Him?

In the middle of His teaching about future times, Jesus once again makes reference to His rejection and suffering. It was to be something that must happen first. Whatever thoughts we have of Christ, and whatever knowledge we may have or not have about the Bible, the cross and Jesus' sacrifice for the penalty of our sins is the one thing that sustains and holds the whole thing together. Paul was quite clear about the centrality of the cross:

Moreover, brethren, I declare to you the gospel which I preached to you, which also you received and in which you stand, by which also you are saved, if you hold fast that word which I preached to you—unless you believed in vain. For I delivered to you first of all that which I also received: that Christ died for our sins according to the Scriptures, and that He was buried, and that He rose again the third day according to the Scriptures. (1 Corinthians 15: 1-4)

At the end of the book of Revelation we read Christ's words, "Surely I am coming quickly." Can we respond "Amen. Even so, come, Lord Jesus."? (Revelation 22: 20)

Luke 18:1-17

1 Then He spoke a parable to them, that men always ought to pray and not lose heart, **2** saying: "There was in a certain city a judge who did not fear God nor regard man. **3** Now there was a widow in that city; and she came to him, saying, 'Get justice for me from my adversary.' **4** And he would not for a while; but afterward he said within himself, 'Though I do not fear God nor regard man, **5** yet because this widow troubles me I will avenge her, lest by her continual coming she weary me.'" **6** Then the Lord said, "Hear what the unjust judge said. **7** And shall God not avenge His own elect who cry out day and night to Him, though He bears long with them? **8** I tell you that He will avenge them speedily. Nevertheless, when the Son of Man comes, will He really find faith on the earth?" **9** Also He spoke this parable to some who trusted in themselves that they were righteous, and despised others: **10** "Two men went up to the temple to pray, one a Pharisee and the other a tax collector. **11** The Pharisee stood and prayed thus with himself, 'God, I thank You that I am not like other men—extortioners, unjust, adulterers, or even as this tax collector. **12** I fast twice a week; I give tithes of all that I possess.' **13** And the tax collector, standing afar off, would not so much as raise *his* eyes to heaven, but beat his breast, saying, 'God, be merciful to me a sinner!' **14** I tell you, this man went down to his house justified *rather* than the other; for everyone who exalts himself will be humbled, and he who humbles himself will be exalted." **15** Then they also brought infants to Him that He might touch them; but when the disciples saw *it,* they rebuked them. **16** But Jesus called them to *Him* and said, "Let the little children come to Me, and do not forbid them; for of such is the kingdom of God. **17** Assuredly, I say to you, whoever does not receive the kingdom of God as a little child will by no means enter it."

This Chapter begins with a story about prayer. How much do we trust God? We all have difficulties which we face day after day, year after year. There may be concerns about health, family breakdown, employment or unemployment or someone who continues to persecute us. We pray about them repeatedly and the problems do not seem to go away. Here, we are invited to be aware that God understands and knows all about it and that one day between now and eternity all will be resolved. We are to commit our lives to Him and trust Him. It is a lesson we all have to learn.

The picture of a pestering widow and an irascible, godless judge, who out of irritation gives in to her request, is there to reassure us that our God understands, cares and is wiser than any flawed human judge.

Because of the human requirement for quick fixes, Jesus asked the pertinent question, "When the Son of Man comes, will He really find faith on the earth?" (v. 8)

It is not by accident that patience or longsuffering is a fruit of the Spirit. (Galatians 5: 22)

Self-righteousness is a contagious disease found amongst the religious and respectable. It can be both obvious and subtle in its presentation. Whatever the presentation, the features and outcomes are clear.

Firstly, prayers are ineffectual if they do not go out to God and remain solely in the mind and head of the speaker. The Pharisee prayed with himself.

Secondly, the speaker was preoccupied with his own goodness, his own achievements and was only too willing to compare himself with others. His self-obsession meant that he had little true appreciation of the holiness of God. He had no understanding as to the state of his own heart. He had no consideration for the man who stood behind him.

We would all do well to heed Jesus' warnings on this issue:

This people honors Me with their lips, But their heart is far from Me. And in vain they worship Me, Teaching as doctrines the commandments of men. (Mark 7: 6-7)

The second man was a hated tax-collector and co-operated with the despised Roman occupiers. He knew he was in need of forgiveness. He did not recite a catalogue of achievements but was humble before God. He asked for mercy and received it. He was not only forgiven, but also became right before God.

The final part of this passage presents a wonderful picture of Jesus' attitude to children. Earlier, we read that Jesus was concerned about the things they were taught. (Luke 17. 2) On this occasion, it is our attitude and a child-like heart that He brings to our attention. At that time, children had no status in that society. Jesus demonstrated their value as God's children and our required mind-set in order to enter the kingdom of God. (v. 17) This is in direct contrast to the Pharisee. (vv. 11-12)

Luke 18:18-34

18 Now a certain ruler asked Him, saying, "Good Teacher, what shall I do to inherit eternal life?" **19** So Jesus said to him, "Why do you call Me good? No one *is* good but One, *that is,* God. **20** You know the commandments: 'Do not commit adultery,' 'Do not murder,' 'Do not steal,' 'Do not bear false witness,' 'Honor your father and your mother.' " **21** And he said, "All these things I have kept from my youth." **22** So when Jesus heard these things, He said to him, "You still lack one thing. Sell all that you have and distribute to the poor, and you will have treasure in heaven; and come, follow Me." **23** But when he heard this, he became very sorrowful, for he was very rich. **24** And when Jesus saw that he became very sorrowful, He said, "How hard it is for those who have riches to enter the kingdom of God! **25** For it is easier for a camel to go through the eye of a needle than for a rich man to enter the kingdom of God." **26** And those who heard it said, "Who then can be saved?" **27** But He said, "The things which are impossible with men are possible with God." **28** Then Peter said, "See, we have left all and followed You." **29** So He said to them, "Assuredly, I say to you, there is no one who has left house or parents or brothers or wife or children, for the sake of the kingdom of God, **30** who shall not receive many times more in this present time, and in the age to come eternal life." **31** Then He took the twelve aside and said to them, "Behold, we are going up to Jerusalem, and all things that are written by the prophets concerning the Son of Man will be accomplished. **32** For He will be delivered to the Gentiles and will be mocked and insulted and spit upon. **33** They will scourge *Him* and kill Him. And the third day He will rise again." **34** But they understood none of these things; this saying was hidden from them, and they did not know the things which were spoken.

The interview with a rich ruler is as informative as it is surprising. In Matthew, he is described as young. (Matthew 19: 22) Unlike those of many others, the young man's question appeared to be sincere. He was more thoughtful than many of his age. In asking his question he prompted other questions that we all ask at some time in one form or another, "What happens when I die? If there is eternal life, how do I achieve it?"

The ruler's address to Jesus as "good teacher", made Jesus give a response to make the man think again. Jesus did not say that He was a sinner. He asked a question to make everyone think about the very person of Jesus. "Why do you call Me good?"

The young man, like many first century teachers, thought it possible to keep the whole Law. It was, he thought, because of this that God rewarded him with riches.

The Law seemed to have become a "tick box exercise". This man thought that he could and did keep it.

Later, the Apostle Paul learnt that it was not possible to keep the Law and that two of its functions are firstly to make us realize that we cannot keep it and, secondly, it drives us to Christ Himself. (Romans 7: 1-12)

Jesus suggested that the young man sell all that he had and follow Him. The young man's riches had become between him and God. Sadly, the young man preferred his riches.

All this confronts us in every age to ask what it really means to follow Christ. It is clear that riches can be a vast hindrance. In the early chapters of Acts, believers divested themselves of much wealth, but kept houses and were self-supporting. The issue that challenges us, is who and what comes first in our lives. Is it our wealth, family, position, comfort, or is it Christ? Does Christ really define who we are? That issue has been faced in the starkest terms in some parts of the world.

"Change religion or die!" Some have chosen Christ rather than change their allegiance.

Jesus' remarks about a rich man and a camel and the eye of a needle (vv.24-27) have prompted many comments about its origin and meaning. The real point is that it is humanly impossible to pass through, but God can change even the proudest heart.

Peter's automatic, self-assertive comments "see we have left all," prompted a comforting response from our Lord. He knows our motives. He knows the secrets of the heart. (Psalm 44: 21) The subject was brought back to the issue of eternal life. (v. 30)

Finally, (vv.31-34) for the seventh time in the Gospel, Jesus talks about His coming death and resurrection. It is easy for us in hindsight to put this in context but for the disciples it was strange and quite contrary to their understanding of a Messiah. The meaning of Isaiah 53 was still closed to them:

Surely He has borne our griefs And carried our sorrows; Yet we esteemed Him stricken, Smitten by God, and afflicted. But He was wounded for our transgressions, He was bruised for our iniquities; The chastisement for our peace was upon Him, And by His stripes we are healed. (Isaiah 53:4-5)

Luke 18:35-43, 19:1-27

35 Then it happened, as He was coming near Jericho, that a certain blind man sat by the road begging. **36** And hearing a multitude passing by, he asked what it meant. **37** So they told him that Jesus of Nazareth was passing by. **38** And he cried out, saying, "Jesus, Son of David, have mercy on me!" **39** Then those who went before warned him that he should be quiet; but he cried out all the more, "Son of David, have mercy on me!" **40** So Jesus stood still and commanded him to be brought to Him. And when he had come near, He asked him, **41** saying, "What do you want Me to do for you?" He said, "Lord, that I may receive my sight." **42** Then Jesus said to him, "Receive your sight; your faith has made you well." **43** And immediately he received his sight, and followed Him, glorifying God. And all the people, when they saw *it*, gave praise to God. **1** Then *Jesus* entered and passed through Jericho. **2** Now behold, *there was* a man named Zacchaeus who was a chief tax collector, and he was rich. **3** And he sought to see who Jesus was, but could not because of the crowd, for he was of short stature. **4** So he ran ahead and climbed up into a sycamore tree to see Him, for He was going to pass that *way*. **5** And when Jesus came to the place, He looked up and saw him, and said to him, "Zacchaeus, make haste and come down, for today I must stay at your house." **6** So he made haste and came down, and received Him joyfully. **7** But when they saw *it*, they all complained, saying, "He has gone to be a guest with a man who is a sinner." **8** Then Zacchaeus stood and said to the Lord, "Look, Lord, I give half of my goods to the poor; and if I have taken anything from anyone by false accusation, I restore fourfold." **9** And Jesus said to him, "Today salvation has come to this house, because he also is a son of Abraham; **10** for the Son of Man has come to seek and to save that which was lost." **11** Now as they heard these things, He spoke another parable, because He was near Jerusalem and because they thought the kingdom of God would appear immediately. **12** Therefore He said: "A certain nobleman went into a far country to receive for himself a kingdom and to return. **13** So he called ten of his servants, delivered to them ten minas, and said to them, 'Do business till I come.' **14** But his citizens hated him, and sent a delegation after him, saying, 'We will not have this *man* to reign over us.' **15** And so it was that when he returned, having received the kingdom, he then commanded these servants, to whom he had given the money, to be called to him, that he might know how much every man had gained by trading. **16** Then came the first, saying, 'Master, your mina has earned ten minas.' **17** And he said to him, 'Well *done,* good servant; because you were faithful in a very little, have authority over ten cities.' **18** And the second came, saying, 'Master, your mina has earned five minas.' **19** Likewise he said to him, 'You also be over five cities.' **20** Then another came, saying, 'Master, here is your mina, which I have kept put away in a handkerchief. **21** For I feared you, because you are an austere man. You collect what you did not deposit, and reap what you did not sow.' **22** And he said to him, 'Out of your own mouth I will judge you, *you* wicked servant. You knew that I was an austere man, collecting what I did not deposit and reaping what I did not sow. **23** Why then did you not put my money in the bank, that at my coming I might have collected it with interest?' **24** And he said to those who stood by, 'Take the mina from him, and give *it* to him who has ten minas.' **25** (But they said to him, 'Master, he has ten minas.') **26** 'For I say to you, that to everyone who has will be given; and from him who does not have, even what he has will be taken away from him. **27** But bring here those enemies of mine, who did not want me to reign over them, and slay *them* before me'."

As Jesus approached and passed through Jericho, He was accompanied by crowds on their way to the Jerusalem feast. Luke gives an atmosphere of a royal procession with a difference. Some of the key figures were not "courtiers" but those from poor and despised backgrounds.

The poor beggar at the side of the road was named by Mark as Bartimaeus. (Mark 10: 46)

We learn, firstly, from this incident that Jesus gave a special place to a man others thought not worthy of consideration. Some would have described him as one of life's losers, but Jesus gave him His complete total attention.

Secondly, the beggar gave Jesus a Messianic title, "Son of David". David was Israel's greatest king, and Bartimaeus gave Jesus the highest title he could utter. Although Jesus did not deny the title, His main thoughts were on the man's needs.

Thirdly, in restoring the man's sight, Jesus asserted the need for authentic faith. Like the one leper who returned, (Luke 17: 18) the healed man gave praise to God. Such a healing and the man's response spread an outpouring of praise of God. (v.43) Genuine heartfelt faith and praise is infectious in the best kind of way. Conversely, self-righteous grumbling is infectious in the worst kind of way.

Jericho was a commercial centre for the production of balsam. Zacchaeus as a despised tax-collector was made rich in the process. The personal details of his stature and the need to climb into a tree give a homely validity to the story. The fact that Jesus called Zacchaeus by name may indicate that the two had met before or it may simply be a demonstration of the omniscience of Jesus. Now was a crunch moment. Zacchaeus could have turned away like the rich ruler, or at last, he could say 'Yes!' He knew that Jesus wanted to put his life on the right track, and Zacchaeus made amends by restoration to those he had once cheated. He made a just disposal of a large part of his fortune. His identity with Jesus and willingness to invite Jesus to share a meal and come into his life brought salvation to the household.

A true descendant of Abraham is one who holds on to the faith that Abraham had. (v. 9) Zacchaeus, a once wealthy, lost and lonely man, was saved. With God, all things are possible.

The parable of the ten Minas or talents was told at a time of high expectation of an imminent earthly political kingdom, similar to the type that Jesus was tempted to set up at the beginning of His ministry. (Luke 4: 5-8)

Jesus spoke of a king who was to depart and then return. The servants were to work and build up responsibilities of service in variously sized projects. The return of the king was associated with rewards. (vv. 16-19) It was sad that one made little use of the gift that was given him.

Spiritually speaking, he could have been given a measure of faith, but he made nothing of it. It was buried by neglect.

The condemnation in verse 27 at the end comes as a disturbing surprise.

Nevertheless, Scripture is full of God's patient forbearance:

But, beloved, do not forget this one thing, that with the Lord one day is as a thousand years, and a thousand years as one day. The Lord is not slack concerning His promise, as some count slackness, but is longsuffering toward us, not willing that any should perish but that all should come to repentance. (2 Peter 3: 8-9)

Many commentators believe that the judgment (v. 27) was fulfilled in AD 70 with the crushing of the first Jewish revolt and the associated fall of Jerusalem. They link the fall to the rejection of Jesus and the desire to establish a politico-religious state.

contempt for master v 21,22.
neglect of responsibility.
dishonest. He has been

Luke 19:28-48

28 When He had said this, He went on ahead, going up to Jerusalem. **29** And it came to pass, when He drew near to Bethphage and Bethany, at the mountain called Olivet, *that* He sent two of His disciples, **30** saying, "Go into the village opposite *you,* where as you enter you will find a colt tied, on which no one has ever sat. Loose it and bring *it here.* **31** And if anyone asks you, 'Why are you loosing *it?*' thus you shall say to him, 'Because the Lord has need of it.'" **32** So those who were sent went their way and found *it* just as He had said to them. **33** But as they were loosing the colt, the owners of it said to them, "Why are you loosing the colt?" **34** And they said, "The Lord has need of him." **35** Then they brought him to Jesus. And they threw their own clothes on the colt, and they set Jesus on him. **36** And as He went, *many* spread their clothes on the road. **37** Then, as He was now drawing near the descent of the Mount of Olives, the whole multitude of the disciples began to rejoice and praise God with a loud voice for all the mighty works they had seen, **38** saying: " 'Blessed *is* the King who comes in the name of the Lord!' Peace in heaven and glory in the highest!" **39** And some of the Pharisees called to Him from the crowd, "Teacher, rebuke Your disciples." **40** But He answered and said to them, "I tell you that if these should keep silent, the stones would immediately cry out." **41** Now as He drew near, He saw the city and wept over it, **42** saying, "If you had known, even you, especially in this your day, the things *that make* for your peace! But now they are hidden from your eyes. **43** For days will come upon you when your enemies will build an embankment around you, surround you and close you in on every side, **44** and level you, and your children within you, to the ground; and they will not leave in you one stone upon another, because you did not know the time of your visitation." **45** Then He went into the temple and began to drive out those who bought and sold in it, **46** saying to them, "It is written, 'My house is a house of prayer,' but you have made it a 'den of thieves.'" **47** And He was teaching daily in the temple. But the chief priests, the scribes, and the leaders of the people sought to destroy Him, **48** and were unable to do anything; for all the people were very attentive to hear Him.

Some have suggested that Jesus had made prior arrangements for

His transport into Jerusalem. The Gospel writers, however, appear to suggest that the obtaining of the colt and the surrounding conversations were linked to royal, divine sovereignty. Just as Jesus knew the thoughts of men, He knew what was to happen, and other Gospel writers link the ride to a prophecy in Zechariah. The picture is of a king yet clothed in humility. (Zechariah 9:9)

At this point, it is worth making some remarks on the kingship of Christ. Up till then Jesus had talked many times about a kingdom. The wise men looked for and found the King of the Jews (Matthew 2:2). Jesus received those who fell at His feet as if to a king. He accepted the title, "Lord." (Luke 17:5) The blind beggar called Him, "Son of David." (Luke 18: 38)

Nevertheless, there was a certain reticence in Jesus. He urged healed people to tell no-one. He withdrew into the mountains to escape the crowds. Even at a mid-point in His ministry some tried to make Him a king. (John 6: 15) As has already been stated, Jesus was concerned about the true motives of many in the crowd.

There was another reason for reticence which is referred to in John's Gospel, more than once and in different contexts. It is stated that His or Mine hour "is not yet come". The ride into Jerusalem was the herald to that hour, when He would suffer many things at the hands of men. Now was the time to accept the title of King. Now His hour had come. Now was the time to put palms and cloaks in the way.

He was not like emperors who were always concerned to feed the appetites of the Roman mob. His kingship is a gracious, just and merciful, eternal kingship. He is a king who died in the place of His people. He does not promise health, wealth, or a job, as if they are entitlements, but He does promise everlasting life and forgiveness. The question has always been, to whom or to what do we give our allegiance?

The Pharisees once again tried to rebuke the king. Jesus gave them an implicit reference to His power and lordship even over nature. (v. 40)

Previously in the parable of the minas, Jesus referred to the future judgment of Israel in stark terms. On the approach to Jerusalem,

He wept over the city. If they had known the peace of God and accepted Jesus, they would not have initiated an ill-considered revolt that led to Jerusalem's eventual destruction in AD 70.

Say to them: 'As I live,' says the Lord GOD, 'I have no pleasure in the death of the wicked, but that the wicked turn from his way and live.' (Ezekiel 33: 11)

The cleansing of the Temple caused controversy then and still does. It was a rare time when Jesus showed anger, but it was, of course, righteous anger. A place of worship and a specific area for Gentiles had been turned into a place of corrupt money-changing and merchandising.

Some have thought that any purchase of books or coffee should be excluded from church premises. That is not referred to in this context unless of course there is associated wrongdoing. The Chapter ends with a note about Jesus' wonderful gift of communication, (v.48) which for the time being delayed the inevitable.

Luke 20:1-26

1 Now it happened on one of those days, as He taught the people in the temple and preached the gospel, *that* the chief priests and the scribes, together with the elders, confronted Him 2 and spoke to Him, saying, "Tell us, by what authority are You doing these things? Or who is he who gave You this authority?" 3 But He answered and said to them, "I also will ask you one thing, and answer Me: 4 The baptism of John—was it from heaven or from men?" 5 And they reasoned among themselves, saying, "If we say, 'From heaven,' He will say, 'Why then did you not believe him?' 6 But if we say, 'From men,' all the people will stone us, for they are persuaded that John was a prophet." 7 So they answered that they did not know where *it was* from. 8 And Jesus said to them, "Neither will I tell you by what authority I do these things." 9 Then He began to tell the people this parable: "A certain man planted a vineyard, leased it to vinedressers, and went into a far country for a long time. 10 Now at vintage-time he sent a servant to the vinedressers, that they might give him some of the fruit of the vineyard. But the vinedressers beat him and sent *him* away empty-handed. 11 Again he sent another servant; and they beat him also, treated *him* shamefully, and sent *him* away empty-handed. 12 And again he sent a third; and they wounded him also and cast *him* out. 13 Then the owner of the vineyard said, 'What shall I do? I will send my beloved son. Probably they will respect *him* when they see him.' 14 But when the vinedressers saw him, they reasoned among themselves, saying, 'This is the heir. Come, let us kill him, that the inheritance may be ours.' 15 So they cast him out of the vineyard and killed *him*. Therefore what will the owner of the vineyard do to them? 16 He will come and destroy those vinedressers and give the vineyard to others." And when they heard *it* they said, "Certainly not!" 17 Then He looked at them and said, "What then is this that is written: 'The stone which the builders rejected has become the chief cornerstone'? 18 Whoever falls on that stone will be broken; but on whomever it falls, it will grind him to powder." 19 And the chief priests and the scribes that very hour sought to lay hands on Him, but they feared the people —for they knew He had spoken this parable against them. 20 So they watched *Him*, and sent spies who pretended to be righteous, that they might seize on His words, in order to deliver Him to the power and the authority of the governor. 21 Then they asked Him, saying, "Teacher, we know that You say and teach rightly, and You do not show personal favoritism, but teach the way of God in truth: 22 Is it lawful

for us to pay taxes to Caesar or not?" **23** But He perceived their craftiness, and said to them, "Why do you test Me? **24** Show Me a denarius. Whose image and inscription does it have?" They answered and said, "Caesar's." **25** And He said to them, "Render therefore to Caesar the things that are Caesar's, and to God the things that are God's." **26** But they could not catch Him in His words in the presence of the people. And they marveled at His answer and kept silent.

A large portion of the Gospels is taken up with the final week of Jesus' life.

Such is its importance! Not only did Jesus come to teach and minister, more importantly, He came to save.

In view of the events of the previous few days, the authorities felt under pressure and were losing control. The first attack came in the form of a question about authority.

In His ministry, Jesus used three devices to answer questions. The first was the direct answer. The second was an answer in the form of a parable and the third was, as on this occasion, to ask a question Himself.

John the Baptist, who had been executed two or so years earlier, was still respected as a prophet by many of the thousands who had been baptized by Him.

He testified that Jesus was the Messiah. So Jesus asked what the chief priests and lawyers thought about the authority of John. That put them on the spot. If they said that he was of God, then they would be asked why they did not listen to him. If they thought that he was not of God, then the crowd would have scorned them.

So the group that had prided themselves of knowing all things religious were silent and not a little humbled.

The question of authority, (v.2) has presented itself in many guises. If there has been innovation or a new invention, those at the top of the profession or trade often feel threatened and ask about credentials of the inventor. Whilst peer review is right and essential, it should not be a disguise for jealousy and point scoring. Young faithful Christians will often find their faith challenged. Whilst none of us is perfect and all of us can learn from criticism, we must remember that the Son of God had to handle difficult people many times.

Churches are particularly prone to ask questions about authority when a new work of God is seen to arise. If a work does not come out from the leadership then it must be suspect! Prayer and humility are necessary to appraise such things.

The meaning of the parable of the tenants was plain to all who heard Jesus. Israel had treated the prophets badly. Many of them had been killed. In this parable, Jesus referred to Himself as God's Son. All who rejected Jesus would be doomed. (v.16) His building metaphor (v.17) also suggested that He was the new temple and that the one in which they were standing would become obsolete.

Jesus was now speaking in plain stark terms. Jesus still offered His hearers an opportunity to respond to Him.

The question of taxes and our allegiance to temporal authority showed the great wisdom of Jesus. In Paul's writings we are urged to pay taxes:

Let every soul be subject to the governing authorities. For there is no authority except from God, and the authorities that exist are appointed by God. Therefore whoever resists the authority resists the ordinance of God, and those who resist will bring judgment on themselves. For rulers are not a terror to good works, but to evil. Do you want to be unafraid of the authority? Do what is good, and you will have praise from the same. For he is God's minister to you for good. But if you do evil, be afraid; for he does not bear the sword in vain; for he is God's minister, an avenger to execute wrath on him who practices evil. Therefore you must be subject, not only because of wrath but also for conscience' sake. For because of this you also pay taxes, for they are God's ministers attending continually to this very thing. Render therefore to all their due: taxes to whom taxes are due, customs to whom customs, fear to whom fear, honor to whom honor. (Romans 13: 1-7)

Although many things appear to belong to Caesar or worldly authority, in fact, everything, ultimately belongs to God.

Luke 20:27-47

27 Then some of the Sadducees, who deny that there is a resurrection, came to *Him* and asked Him, 28 saying: "Teacher, Moses wrote to us *that* if a man's brother dies, having a wife, and he dies without children, his brother should take his wife and raise up offspring for his brother. 29 Now there were seven brothers. And the first took a wife, and died without children. 30 And the second took her as wife, and he died childless. 31 Then the third took her, and in like manner the seven also; and they left no children, and died. 32 Last of all the woman died also. 33 Therefore, in the resurrection, whose wife does she become? For all seven had her as wife." 34 Jesus answered and said to them, "The sons of this age marry and are given in marriage. 35 But those who are counted worthy to attain that age, and the resurrection from the dead, neither marry nor are given in marriage; 36 nor can they die anymore, for they are equal to the angels and are sons of God, being sons of the resurrection. 37 But even Moses showed in the *burning* bush *passage* that the dead are raised, when he called the Lord 'the God of Abraham, the God of Isaac, and the God of Jacob.' 38 For He is not the God of the dead but of the living, for all live to Him." 39 Then some of the scribes answered and said, "Teacher, You have spoken well." 40 But after that they dared not question Him anymore. 41 And He said to them, "How can they say that the Christ is the Son of David? 42 Now David himself said in the Book of Psalms: 'The LORD said to my Lord, "Sit at My right hand, 43 Till I make Your enemies Your footstool."' 44 Therefore David calls Him 'Lord'; how is He then his Son?" 45 Then, in the hearing of all the people, He said to His disciples, 46 "Beware of the scribes, who desire to go around in long robes, love greetings in the marketplaces, the best seats in the synagogues, and the best places at feasts, 47 who devour widows' houses, and for a pretense make long prayers. These will receive greater condemnation."

Sadducees were part of the temple aristocracy. In a way, they were the equivalent to modern liberal scholars. They believed that only the first five books of the Bible were inspired. They did not believe in the presence of angels or the resurrection. The Pharisees believed in the other books of the Old Testament and in the idea of resurrection.

Richard Dawkins, the biologist, was in a debate with John Lennox, the Christian mathematician apologist. When John Lennox spoke about the resurrection of Jesus, Dawkins said that the resurrection was unfitting for the Universe. It was as if the Universe itself had a personality. Clearly, he wanted to decry all the historic evidence in support of the resurrection of Jesus.

We have a foundation on which a Christian can base a belief in the resurrection, namely the resurrection of Jesus Himself.

The Sadducees sought to trap Jesus by describing an imaginary absurd scenario of seven brothers who in turn had married the same woman. Jesus did not return a question or tell a parable, He answered the question directly. His answer spoke of the resurrection and the post-resurrection state, and the existence of angels. He asserted again that this life is not all there is. He reinforced this idea with a comment (v. 37) from one of the books they believed in. (Exodus 3:6)

Jesus had answered all His critics. That was the last question asked by His opposition before His trial.

Then Jesus asked a pertinent question about the nature of the Messiah. Earlier in Jericho the healed man referred to Jesus as the "Son of David". In a way, that title did not give true status to the Messiah. Jesus, by quoting David, elevated the status to something much more. He is at the right hand of the Father. (Psalm 110:1) Men have thought too little of Christ but no-one has thought too highly of Him.

Finally, Jesus gave a warning about the character of some religious leaders. Such a warning is as relevant today as it was then. There are those that seek the greeting and respect of all. They love to occupy important seats in church and are known for their long prayers. They love their flowing robes. These people are not confined to one church. No matter how simple or complicated the ordering of the church is, there will be a risk of people who exploit their position for their own ends. Jesus then included in the catalogue those who exploit the poor, in particular, the widows. Such men have their hearts in the wrong place. They will receive punishment and loss. (v. 47)

Before leaving this passage it is worth making a note about anti-Semitism. Anti-Semitism has been present in all societies and has stained the Christian church. It has led to extremes of hatred and violence.

From reading the Gospels and Acts, a bleak picture is presented of the main Jewish authority. Their religion was corrupt and their failure to believe in Jesus was all too clear. Their persecution of the early church was intense.

Nevertheless, the early believers were all Jews. Paul, in spite of severe persecution, expressed a love for the Jews and so should we. He wrote a large section of Romans to put into perspective a right attitude towards the Jews. Here are some quotes from chapters 10 and 11:

Brethren, my heart's desire and prayer to God for Israel is that they may be saved. For I bear them witness that they have a zeal for God, but not according to knowledge. (Romans 10: 1-2)

I say then, has God cast away His people? Certainly not! For I also am an Israelite, of the seed of Abraham, of the tribe of Benjamin. God has not cast away His people whom He foreknew. (Romans 11: 1-2)

There is no place for anti-Semitism amongst God's people.

Luke 21:1-37

1 And He looked up and saw the rich putting their gifts into the treasury, 2 and He saw also a certain poor widow putting in two mites. 3 So He said, "Truly I say to you that this poor widow has put in more than all; 4 for all these out of their abundance have put in offerings for God, but she out of her poverty put in all the livelihood that she had." 5 Then, as some spoke of the temple, how it was adorned with beautiful stones and donations, He said, 6 "These things which you see—the days will come in which not *one* stone shall be left upon another that shall not be thrown down." 7 So they asked Him, saying, "Teacher, but when will these things be? And what sign *will there be* when these things are about to take place?" 8 And He said: "Take heed that you not be deceived. For many will come in My name, saying, 'I am *He*,' and, 'The time has drawn near.' Therefore do not go after them. 9 But when you hear of wars and commotions, do not be terrified; for these things must come to pass first, but the end *will* not *come* immediately." 10 Then He said to them, "Nation will rise against nation, and kingdom against kingdom. 11 And there will be great earthquakes in various places, and famines and pestilences; and there will be fearful sights and great signs from heaven. 12 But before all these things, they will lay their hands on you and persecute *you*, delivering *you* up to the synagogues and prisons. You will be brought before kings and rulers for My name's sake. 13 But it will turn out for you as an occasion for testimony. 14 Therefore settle *it* in your hearts not to meditate beforehand on what you will answer; 15 for I will give you a mouth and wisdom which all your adversaries will not be able to contradict or resist. 16 You will be betrayed even by parents and brothers, relatives and friends; and they will put *some* of you to death. 17 And you will be hated by all for My name's sake. 18 But not a hair of your head shall be lost. 19 By your patience possess your souls. 20 But when you see Jerusalem surrounded by armies, then know that its desolation is near. 21 Then let those who are in Judea flee to the mountains, let those who are in the midst of her depart, and let not those who are in the country enter her. 22 For these are the days of vengeance, that all things which are written may be fulfilled. 23 But woe to those who are pregnant and to those who are nursing babies in those days! For there will be great distress in the land and wrath upon this people. 24 And they will fall by the edge of the sword, and be led away captive into all nations. And Jerusalem will be trampled by Gentiles until the times of the Gentiles are fulfilled. 25 And there will be signs in

the sun, in the moon, and in the stars; and on the earth distress of nations, with perplexity, the sea and the waves roaring; **26** men's hearts failing them from fear and the expectation of those things which are coming on the earth, for the powers of the heavens will be shaken. **27** Then they will see the Son of Man coming in a cloud with power and great glory. **28** Now when these things begin to happen, look up and lift up your heads, because your redemption draws near." **29** Then He spoke to them a parable: "Look at the fig tree, and all the trees. **30** When they are already budding, you see and know for yourselves that summer is now near. **31** So you also, when you see these things happening, know that the kingdom of God is near. **32** Assuredly, I say to you, this generation will by no means pass away till all things take place. **33** Heaven and earth will pass away, but My words will by no means pass away. **34** But take heed to yourselves, lest your hearts be weighed down with carousing, drunkenness, and cares of this life, and that Day come on you unexpectedly. **35** For it will come as a snare on all those who dwell on the face of the whole earth. **36** Watch therefore, and pray always that you may be counted worthy to escape all these things that will come to pass, and to stand before the Son of Man." **37** And in the daytime He was teaching in the temple, but at night He went out and stayed on the mountain called Olivet. **38** Then early in the morning all the people came to Him in the temple to hear Him.

Many sermons have been preached on the widow's offering. They have rightly emphasized her devotion and the fact that she gave more than the other wealthy contributors because that was all she had. In my experience, churches from deprived areas give comparatively more than those from wealthy parts. However, in light of what was said in the previous chapter, (v.47) a more nuanced interpretation could be put on the incident.

In the previous chapter, Jesus condemned the authorities because of their exploitation of widows and their demands on them. Widows seem to have had few rights and following the deaths of their husbands, lost their houses and had to give large segments of their resources into the treasury. In other words, she gave her gift because of the unjust moral force that was put upon her in her vulnerable state. God would not expect anyone to be totally impoverished because of the demands of giving. A wise church urges all to give and yet, no-one, particularly those with little means or debt problems, should be put under emotional pressure.

The appearance of a great building or cathedral can arouse many types of emotion. The ability of architects, builders, sculptors and artists fills one with a sense of awe, wonder and admiration. Some would describe it as a spiritual experience. Such were the feelings of the disciples as they walked around Herod's great temple in Jerusalem.

Although the temple was dedicated to God, it was done so in vain because, as Jesus had warned previously, destruction was to fall upon it at the hands of the Romans. Jesus also linked this to the end of the age which would come about millennia later. The connection of near events to more distant ones is a prophetic device often used in Scripture.

Jesus brought to our attention the following:

Firstly, there will be in various areas false Christs or Messiahs who will appeal to many. Some will wield terrifying influence, but once again Jesus encouraged us not to be taken in and not to be afraid.

Secondly, we see progress in so many spheres and we seek and justifiably pray for peace within and between nations. Although there have been and will be times of comparative peace, for which we must be thankful, there has been and always will be tension and conflict between peoples and individuals. "Nation will rise against nation." (v.10)

Thirdly, there will continue to be natural disasters. We have wiped out smallpox, and have treatments for many of the scourges that have afflicted humankind. We have achieved much in medical science, but we will always have to cope with diseases and ill-health.

Fourthly, there will always be persecution of Christians. From this passage it is clear that those undergoing such ordeals will have a sense of closeness to God. He will be their strength. He will inspire the right words to say, even in the most extreme moments.

Jesus then returned to the theme of the fall of Israel and the believers' response. (v.28) It has been stated by early Christian writers that, because of the Lord's prophecy, (v.20) numbers of Christians fled from Jerusalem and Judea. They escaped east over Jordan prior to the attack on Jerusalem in AD 70.

Many have expressed doubt about the second coming of Christ and the sudden final judgment. Yet, every other prophecy about Jesus has been fulfilled. "Watch and pray, (v. 36) Christ will come again!"

Luke 22:1-13

1 Now the Feast of Unleavened Bread drew near, which is called Passover. **2** And the chief priests and the scribes sought how they might kill Him, for they feared the people. **3** Then Satan entered Judas, surnamed Iscariot, who was numbered among the twelve. **4** So he went his way and conferred with the chief priests and captains, how he might betray Him to them. **5** And they were glad, and agreed to give him money. **6** So he promised and sought opportunity to betray Him to them in the absence of the multitude. **7** Then came the Day of Unleavened Bread, when the Passover must be killed. **8** And He sent Peter and John, saying, "Go and prepare the Passover for us, that we may eat." **9** So they said to Him, "Where do You want us to prepare?" **10** And He said to them, "Behold, when you have entered the city, a man will meet you carrying a pitcher of water; follow him into the house which he enters. **11** Then you shall say to the master of the house, 'The Teacher says to you, "Where is the guest room where I may eat the Passover with My disciples?"' **12** Then he will show you a large, furnished upper room; there make ready." **13** So they went and found it just as He had said to them, and they prepared the Passover.

As the chief priests plotted against Jesus, something went on in the mind of Judas Iscariot. Writers, dramatists, and Bible commentators have tried to get into his mind. Some have tried to rationalize his betrayal as an attempt by a well-meaning man to force the hand of Jesus to become established as a religious political leader. I believe that this view is at best naïve. There was something wrong with Judas from the beginning. There was a remarkable forbearance of Jesus in that He put up with it for so long.

He objected to the lavish devotion given to Jesus when costly perfume was poured over Him, and cynically suggested that the money should be given to the poor. (John 12: 4) Judas administered the finance of the group and one Gospel writer indicated that he took some of the cash for himself. In other words, he had his fingers in the till. (John 12:6) It appears that his desire for monetary gain twisted his appreciation of Jesus' miracles and ministry. Clearly, Judas' desire for cash made him disillusioned. Judas' repeated resistance of what was right laid himself open to worse evil and subsequent yielding to the devil. (v.3)

The story of Judas Iscariot teaches us two main points. Firstly, there are people in Christian organizations whose main loyalty is not to Christ but to their own selfish benefit. If one of the twelve was a traitor, then we should not be surprised if such people infiltrate the church.

Secondly, it shows how a moral flaw can grow to such an extent that conscience becomes hardened. It is a good thing to set aside time and occasionally examine our own motivation.

Thirdly, let us pray for and thank God for treasurers and finance directors who are godly and honest.

Jesus was aware of Judas' consultation with the authorities. This did not divert His mission as He prepared for the Passover meal. Luke makes a poignant comment that the Passover lamb had to be sacrificed. (v.7) The implication is that the sacrifice would be Jesus. Although the sacrifice commemorated the escape from the deaths that afflicted the Egyptian firstborn centuries before, (Exodus 11-12) the sacrifice was also about the forgiveness of sins which Jesus made once and for all. (Hebrews 9:28)

Again, Jesus may have been involved in some planning of the arrangements about the Passover meal or this may be another example of His supernatural knowledge. We do not read much about administration in the Gospels, but here we have an example of the importance of sound administration. Administration sounds secular, and is often relegated to second place, not only in the church but also in other organizations. How often do those working in professions and trades speak negatively about "the administrators"? Good administration is invaluable and needs to be recognized. In fact, administration is spoken of in the New Testament as a spiritual gift. (1 Corinthians 12: 28, Titus 1: 5) Let us pray that God will direct and help us in all our planning, and thank God for those who are employed in this vital task.

Luke 22:14-30

14 When the hour had come, He sat down, and the twelve apostles with Him. **15** Then He said to them, "With *fervent* desire I have desired to eat this Passover with you before I suffer; **16** for I say to you, I will no longer eat of it until it is fulfilled in the kingdom of God." **17** Then He took the cup, and gave thanks, and said, "Take this and divide *it* among yourselves; **18** for I say to you, I will not drink of the fruit of the vine until the kingdom of God comes." **19** And He took bread, gave thanks and broke *it*, and gave *it* to them, saying, "This is My body which is given for you; do this in remembrance of Me." **20** Likewise He also *took* the cup after supper, saying, "This cup *is* the new covenant in My blood, which is shed for you. **21** But behold, the hand of My betrayer *is* with Me on the table. **22** And truly the Son of Man goes as it has been determined, but woe to that man by whom He is betrayed!" **23** Then they began to question among themselves, which of them it was who would do this thing. **24** Now there was also a dispute among them, as to which of them should be considered the greatest. **25** And He said to them, "The kings of the Gentiles exercise lordship over them, and those who exercise authority over them are called 'benefactors.' **26** But not so *among* you; on the contrary, he who is greatest among you, let him be as the younger, and he who governs as he who serves. **27** For who *is* greater, he who sits at the table, or he who serves? *Is* it not he who sits at the table? Yet I am among you as the One who serves. **28** But you are those who have continued with Me in My trials. **29** And I bestow upon you a kingdom, just as My Father bestowed *one* upon Me, **30** that you may eat and drink at My table in My kingdom, and sit on thrones judging the twelve tribes of Israel."

The Lord's Supper is included in all four Gospel accounts and Paul's First Epistle to the Corinthians. Three Gospels and the Epistle refer to the taking of bread and wine. We are given instruction to do this in memory of our Lord's suffering and sacrifice, when He bore the penalty for our sin. His crucifixion was for the remission of sins.

When Jesus said, "This is My body, "(v. 19) nearly all Protestants believe that it should be understood as, "This represents My body." It is a very reasonable conclusion from the text because the languages that Jesus spoke, Hebrew and Aramaic, do not have the verb, "represent". For example, when Jesus said, "I am the door," or "I am the vine," this was meant figuratively. The same thing could also be said in reference to the cup.

The Lord's Supper is a thankful memorial of Jesus' death until He comes again. It should also signify our unity with Christ and all of God's people. As we share in the bread and wine, we feed on Him in our hearts by faith.

The cup of blessing which we bless, is it not the communion of the blood of Christ? The bread which we break, is it not the communion of the body of Christ? For we, though many, are one bread and one body; for we all partake of that one bread. (1 Corinthians 10: 16-17)

These few words barely begin to be an adequate appraisal of the Lord's Supper. Sadly as well as being a source of unity, it has also been a cause of division and persecution.

Luke appears to indicate that even at this moment of fellowship, Judas, the betrayer was with them.

The twelve questioned at first who might betray Jesus and then there was a dispute, as to who should be the greatest. Matthew and Mark place the dispute on another occasion. It could have reared its head again and it appears that they had not learnt from the previous incident.

Although other commentators do not refer to this, it could be placed here because Luke, perhaps unwittingly, wrote prophetically about the later divisions in the church over communion.

If it is believed that the bread and wine truly become the body and blood of Christ, and only a priest can preside over the sacrament, then that gives the priesthood enormous potential spiritual and emotional power over the congregation. The Roman Church has exercised power of this nature in the past. It is a more complex situation than that just described, but it is a great danger. The Roman Church is not the only group to have abused power and trust, it has happened in other churches too. Such churches ultimately damage the cause of the Gospel.

Our Lord taught us here a crucial lesson about service and responsibility. Not only has the abuse of power taken place in the church, it happens in all walks of life, (v.25) including amongst surgeons and physicians!

As we approach the Lord's Table, we should examine our hearts and confess our sins. We are privileged to receive this sacrament with great joy and blessing.

Let us remind ourselves that to have responsibility and authority amongst God's people should be accompanied by humility and a desire to serve, as Jesus did. (John 13: 3-17)

Finally, to walk with Jesus is to share in His trials. Jesus' words about judging the twelve tribes of Israel (v.30) are difficult to comprehend. Again, it is an area where we should exercise humility rather than dogmatism. It could be understood that the example of faith in Jesus the Messiah is in marked contrast and a judgment to many in Israel.

He was in the world, and the world was made through Him, and the world did not know Him. He came to His own, and His own did not receive Him. But as many as received Him, to them He gave the right to become children of God, to those who believe in His name: who were born, not of blood, nor of the will of the flesh, nor of the will of man, but of God. (John 1: 10-13)

Luke 22:31-38

31 And the Lord said, "Simon, Simon! Indeed, Satan has asked for you, that he may sift *you* as wheat. **32** But I have prayed for you, that your faith should not fail; and when you have returned to *Me*, strengthen your brethren." **33** But he said to Him, "Lord, I am ready to go with You, both to prison and to death." **34** Then He said, "I tell you, Peter, the rooster shall not crow this day before you will deny three times that you know Me." **35** And He said to them, "When I sent you without money bag, knapsack, and sandals, did you lack anything?" So they said, "Nothing." **36** Then He said to them, "But now, he who has a money bag, let him take *it,* and likewise a knapsack; and he who has no sword, let him sell his garment and buy one. **37** For I say to you that this which is written must still be accomplished in Me: 'And He was numbered with the transgressors.' For the things concerning Me have an end." **38** So they said, "Lord, look, here *are* two swords." And He said to them, "It is enough."

We learn from these telling verses much about our lives and the type of world that we inhabit.

Firstly, we note the constant presence of evil, Satan, and the temptations we face all too frequently. The reality of Satan is nothing but clear as we look around the evil in the world. Peter, who was to deny his Lord, later referred to Satan as a "roaring lion, seeking whom he may devour." (1 Peter 5:8) We must never treat lightly the reality of the devil.

Secondly, we note that the grace of God is more superior than the machinations of the evil one. We have a great High Priest in Heaven (Hebrews 4: 14-16) who will never let us go even if we fail:

And if anyone sins, we have an Advocate with the Father, Jesus Christ the righteous. And He Himself is the propitiation for our sins, and not for ours only but also for the whole world. (1 John 2: 1-2)

We all experience disappointment and failure. Some of the great characters of the Bible, Moses, David and Peter, let God and themselves down badly. God did not give up on them, and if we desire it, He will not give up on us.

Thirdly, we note the misplaced self-sufficiency and power of the human spirit when Peter declared that he would be prepared to go to prison and even die. (v. 33) This power of the human spirit has been celebrated in the poem *Invictus,* by the Victorian poet, William Henley:

> *Beyond this place of wrath and tears*
> *Looms but the Horror of the shade,*
> *And yet the menace of the years*
> *Finds, and shall find me, unafraid.*
>
> *It matters not how strait the gate,*
> *How charged with punishments the scroll,*
> *I am the master of my fate:*
> *I am the captain of my soul.*

Great as human achievements have been, the vulnerability of humanity is more than evident. It is a false bravery that over-celebrates human triumphs and curses the night. We will one day die. We will all have to give an account before God. That is a time when we will not be able to rely on our successes for salvation, but on God's grace and mercy alone.

Jesus knows our personalities better than we do. In His prophetic utterance about Peter's denial, (v. 34) He brushed away Peter's brave protest.

Verses 34 onwards denote the increasing tension and the unjust death that Jesus must suffer. The Son of God, the Saviour of the world, who did His Father's will and acted out of compassion for the lost, was to be treated like a murderous criminal! (v. 37)

From then on, Jesus advised that we must make wise provision and planning in the work of God and the spreading of the Gospel. His words about buying a sword seem strange, but even Christian men and women sometimes require the help of security services. There is a right balance between wise provision on one hand

and, on the other, the sovereign protection that God gives to His servants.

The disciples were too literal and rather naïve to suggest that two swords were a sufficient requirement. Jesus' words, "It is enough," as we shall see later, were dismissive and ironic.

Luke 22:39-53

39 Coming out, He went to the Mount of Olives, as He was accustomed, and His disciples also followed Him. **40** When He came to the place, He said to them, "Pray that you may not enter into temptation." **41** And He was withdrawn from them about a stone's throw, and He knelt down and prayed, **42** saying, "Father, if it is Your will, take this cup away from Me; nevertheless not My will, but Yours, be done." **43** Then an angel appeared to Him from heaven, strengthening Him. **44** And being in agony, He prayed more earnestly. Then His sweat became like great drops of blood falling down to the ground. **45** When He rose up from prayer, and had come to His disciples, He found them sleeping from sorrow. **46** Then He said to them, "Why do you sleep? Rise and pray, lest you enter into temptation." **47** And while He was still speaking, behold, a multitude; and he who was called Judas, one of the twelve, went before them and drew near to Jesus to kiss Him. **48** But Jesus said to him, "Judas, are you betraying the Son of Man with a kiss?" **49** When those around Him saw what was going to happen, they said to Him, "Lord, shall we strike with the sword?" **50** And one of them struck the servant of the high priest and cut off his right ear. **51** But Jesus answered and said, "Permit even this." And He touched his ear and healed him. **52** Then Jesus said to the chief priests, captains of the temple, and the elders who had come to Him, "Have you come out, as against a robber, with swords and clubs? **53** When I was with you daily in the temple, you did not try to seize Me. But this is your hour, and the power of darkness."

The garden on the Mount of Olives is a quiet, pleasant place to spend an evening. These verses should be read with thoughtful reverence. Jesus knew what was going to happen and why His coming crucifixion was necessary. He was both fully God and fully man. During His ministry there were times when His divinity was evident and times when His humanity came to the surface. In the garden we see His humanity. He knew He would face physical pain and suffering. He also knew that in becoming sin for us (2 Corinthians 5: 21) He would face spiritual separation from His Father.

The sweating of drops of blood or hematidrosis is a well-recognized, if rare, medical phenomenon. It is not well-understood but it is possible that the acute spasm and subsequent dilatation of the blood vessels to the sweat glands causes damage to the walls of those blood vessels. Blood then leaks out into the sweat. The spasm of the blood vessels is caused by chemical mediators released when the person is under severe stress. Hematidrosis has been described in those who face imminent death.

In examining this ordeal, we learn two things about Jesus which are examples for us.

Firstly, He knelt in prayer. We should always bring things to God in prayer but God also welcomes us in our troubles and in times of crisis. Some have erroneously given the impression that Christians are immune from crisis and tribulation. They could not be more wrong.

Secondly, He prayed that His Father's will be done. He committed Himself totally to God's plan and providence. If we do this with an honest heart, then God promises a special comfort for such times. It may not be as visible as an angel but nevertheless just as real.

The disciples were in sorrow about imminent uncertainty concerning the future. Instead of standing with Jesus in prayer, they had fallen asleep. It shows how unreliable the disciples were over so many things and yet Jesus knew, even then, He had not been mistaken in His choice. He knew the end from the beginning. These were the ones who through the power of the Holy Spirit would turn the world upside down. (Acts 17: 6)

The arrival of the priests, elders and the temple guard caught Jesus alone with His disciples. Judas greeted Jesus with a kiss. Even at the moment of betrayal, Judas appeared plausible. Sadly, those who are enemies of the Gospel can sound welcoming and well meaning.

The reaction of Peter – "one of them" – was impulsive. He was three centimetres from being a murderer. Jesus healed the high priest's servant in the absence of faith because Peter's action (John 18: 10) was contrary to His teaching.

It is salutary to remind ourselves that much of the Bible has been written by those involved in homicide. Moses may have been acting in a judicial capacity but he took the law into his own hands when he slew an Egyptian. (Exodus 2:12) David was responsible for the death of Uriah. (2 Samuel 11:15) Peter could have been convicted of attempted murder. Paul shared a common purpose with those who stoned Stephen. (Acts 8:1) Such a catalogue demonstrates the mercy and grace of God in that God was able to forgive and use such men as these. When faced with his actions, David wrote:

> *Have mercy upon me, O God,*
> *According to Your lovingkindness;*
> *According to the multitude of Your tender mercies,*
> *Blot out my transgressions.*
> *Wash me thoroughly from my iniquity,*
> *And cleanse me from my sin....*
>
> *Create in me a clean heart, O God,*
> *And renew a steadfast spirit within me.*
> *Do not cast me away from Your presence,*
> *And do not take Your Holy Spirit from me.*
> *(Psalm 51: 1-2, 10-11)*

It was something Paul never forgot when he described himself as the chief of sinners. (1 Timothy 1: 15)

Verse 53 tells us that the forces of darkness would strive to defeat God's plan of salvation. We can remind ourselves that even when darkness appears to reign and things are at their worst, God's sovereignty is still at work and He has the ultimate victory.

Luke 22:54-71

54 Having arrested Him, they led *Him* and brought Him into the high priest's house. But Peter followed at a distance. **55** Now when they had kindled a fire in the midst of the courtyard and sat down together, Peter sat among them. **56** And a certain servant girl, seeing him as he sat by the fire, looked intently at him and said, "This man was also with Him." **57** But he denied Him, saying, "Woman, I do not know Him." **58** And after a little while another saw him and said, "You also are of them." But Peter said, "Man, I am not!" **59** Then after about an hour had passed, another confidently affirmed, saying, "Surely this *fellow* also was with Him, for he is a Galilean." **60** But Peter said, "Man, I do not know what you are saying!" Immediately, while he was still speaking, the rooster crowed. **61** And the Lord turned and looked at Peter. Then Peter remembered the word of the Lord, how He had said to him, "Before the rooster crows, you will deny Me three times." **62** So Peter went out and wept bitterly. **63** Now the men who held Jesus mocked Him and beat Him. **64** And having blindfolded Him, they struck Him on the face and asked Him, saying, "Prophesy! Who is the one who struck You?" **65** And many other things they blasphemously spoke against Him. **66** As soon as it was day, the elders of the people, both chief priests and scribes, came together and led Him into their council, saying, **67** "If You are the Christ, tell us." But He said to them, "If I tell you, you will by no means believe. **68** And if I also ask *you*, you will by no means answer Me or let *Me* go. **69** Hereafter the Son of Man will sit on the right hand of the power of God." **70** Then they all said, "Are You then the Son of God?" So He said to them, "You *rightly say* that I am." **71** And they said, "What further testimony do we need? For we have heard it ourselves from His own mouth."

Jesus was under arrest and submitted voluntarily to the power of the High Priest's soldiers.

The story of Peter's denial is instructive to the whole world. If Christianity were a made-up story, as atheists insist it is, then the Gospel writers would not have chosen this unflattering episode about one of the leading apostles. It is hardly the sort of material that would have been included in a treatise to promote a fable.

Peter had been given special privileges. He had left his fishing business. He had been a close witness of Jesus' teaching, behaviour and miracles. He was one of three who had observed the raising of Jairus' daughter and the Transfiguration.

Here we notice an aspect of human character that exists in all of us. Whilst with the group, Peter was boisterous in his self-confidence. He would not betray Jesus. He was ready to go to death. When with the group and carrying a sword, he attacked the arrest party in the garden. When alone amidst people who were hostile, self-preservation came to the surface. When we are on our own, we are often prepared to do anything to preserve our own skins. This is why the military like to work in groups and companies organize bonding sessions. We tend to be selfish when we are on our own.

Peter did not heed our Lord's invitation to pray that evening, and became vulnerable to criticism. Christians need to be close to Christ in prayer, and so when confronted with challenges about our faith, we know we are not alone. At that point, we will have the courage to say, "Yes, I am a believer," because He gives us the strength to do so.

We see in this passage, the grace of God. Jesus looked at Peter. We are not told what kind of expression was in that look, but we do know that Jesus was the one that acted in love, even in His own crisis.

Peter went out and wept bitterly. It demonstrates the content of his own heart. He could have left, shrugged his shoulders and thought that it was just one of those things. The fact that he wept was an indication that his real loyalty was to Jesus, although at the same time the world seemed to be falling around him. His was a remorse that led to true repentance, (2 Corinthians 7: 10) unlike that of Judas (Matthew 27: 3-5). Later through God's kindness and forbearance, Peter was completely restored.

After this, the text moves back to Jesus. It shows how sinful men treated Christ and the loss of discipline by the guard. Soldiers can exert great power over people and we often hear of abuse towards prisoners and civilians. It is such an easy mind-set that officers sometimes ignore it and may lose control of their men. In this case there was no restraint in the abuse directed towards the Son of God.

There were a number of trials and interrogations in the short time following Jesus' arrest. Luke recorded four of them. The first trial described by Luke was about two main questions.

Firstly, Is Jesus the Messiah of Israel? Jesus initially refused to answer that question, since the answer was evident in His ministry and admitted miracles. His accusers were not genuine enquirers but wanted to find some means of getting rid of Jesus. Jesus' reply (v. 69) was in fact, "Yes", as He referred to the divine title, "Son of Man". (Daniel 7: 13-14)

Secondly, the follow up question, "Are You then the Son of God?" leads on from the first. Jesus replied in the affirmative. (v. 70) They did not examine the overwhelming evidence about the nature of Christ's person or want to hear defence witnesses, the court rushed to a verdict of guilt. It needs to be said that the world can be in no doubt about the claims of Jesus as to who He is. His identity is obvious!

Luke 23:1-25

1 Then the whole multitude of them arose and led Him to Pilate. 2 And they began to accuse Him, saying, "We found this *fellow* perverting the nation, and forbidding to pay taxes to Caesar, saying that He Himself is Christ, a King." 3 Then Pilate asked Him, saying, "Are You the King of the Jews?" He answered him and said, "*It is as* you say." 4 So Pilate said to the chief priests and the crowd, "I find no fault in this Man." 5 But they were the more fierce, saying, "He stirs up the people, teaching throughout all Judea, beginning from Galilee to this place." 6 When Pilate heard of Galilee, he asked if the Man were a Galilean. 7 And as soon as he knew that He belonged to Herod's jurisdiction, he sent Him to Herod, who was also in Jerusalem at that time. 8 Now when Herod saw Jesus, he was exceedingly glad; for he had desired for a long *time* to see Him, because he had heard many things about Him, and he hoped to see some miracle done by Him. 9 Then he questioned Him with many words, but He answered him nothing. 10 And the chief priests and scribes stood and vehemently accused Him. 11 Then Herod, with his men of war, treated Him with contempt and mocked *Him,* arrayed Him in a gorgeous robe, and sent Him back to Pilate. 12 That very day Pilate and Herod became friends with each other, for previously they had been at enmity with each other. 13 Then Pilate, when he had called together the chief priests, the rulers, and the people, 14 said to them, "You have brought this Man to me, as one who misleads the people. And indeed, having examined *Him* in your presence, I have found no fault in this Man concerning those things of which you accuse Him; 15 no, neither did Herod, for I sent you back to him; and indeed nothing deserving of death has been done by Him. 16 I will therefore chastise Him and release *Him*" 17 (for it was necessary for him to release one to them at the feast). 18 And they all cried out at once, saying, "Away with this *Man,* and release to us Barabbas"— 19 who had been thrown into prison for a certain rebellion made in the city, and for murder. 20 Pilate, therefore, wishing to release Jesus, again called out to them. 21 But they shouted, saying, "Crucify *Him,* crucify Him!" 22 Then he said to them the third time, "Why, what evil has He done? I have found no reason for death in Him. I will therefore chastise Him and let *Him* go." 23 But they were insistent, demanding with loud voices that He be crucified. And the voices of these men and of the chief priests prevailed. 24 So Pilate gave sentence that it should be as they requested. 25 And he

> released to them the one they requested, who for rebellion and murder had been thrown into prison; but he delivered Jesus to their will.

The authorities wanted to get rid of Jesus as soon as possible and brought Him to the Roman procurator since Pontius Pilate could alone pronounce the death penalty. The Jewish assembly touched on an issue that they knew Pilate would be interested in. It concerned Jesus' claims in relation to Caesar. They lied in that Jesus had already granted taxes to Caesar. Pilate was not convinced that Jesus was a threat to Roman rule and so he tried to pass on the issue to Herod, the one who was responsible for the execution of John the Baptist.

Herod was a corrupt character. He had an interest in religion and had discussions with John the Baptist. The world contains many who declare an interest in faith, but do not consider it relevant to their situation. He was pleased because he had heard so much about Jesus, and at one stage feared Him and tried to remove Him. (Luke 13:31) He wanted to see a miracle as we might want to see a conjuring trick. Herod was too well-fixed in his position to give any kind of allegiance to Christ. Jesus refused to answer questions from the blasphemous ruler. In the Bible, we are told that Jesus went out to save that which was lost. It is worth noting that He did not go running after men whose minds were utterly closed. With many others who have no place for Christ in their lives, Herod joined in the abuse, and returned Jesus to Pilate. Peter never forgot the utter meekness of the Saviour:

But when you do good and suffer, if you take it patiently, this is commendable before God. For to this you were called, because Christ also suffered for us, leaving us an example, that you should follow His steps:

"Who committed no sin, Nor was deceit found in His mouth"; who, when He was reviled, did not revile in return; when He suffered, He did not threaten, but committed Himself to Him who judges righteously; (1 Peter 2:20-23)

Verse 12 denotes how men who once loathed one another became friends because of their mutual antipathy to Christ. The key question as far as Pilate was concerned was this – Was Jesus a threat to order? Was He the leader of a rebellion? The answer to both those questions was "No!" He tried to release Jesus, and more than once tried to appeal to reason. Eventually, Pilate buckled under the verbal pressure of the authorities and the surrounding partisan crowd. He committed an injustice by releasing a convicted murderer and handed over an innocent man to be crucified. In the end, he did that which was politically expedient. Let us pray that our politicians and indeed all of us will choose just courses of action rather than those which are convenient. The telling phrase in the passage is, and he surrendered "Jesus to their will." (v. 25)

Verse 22 states that Pilate had Jesus punished. Other Gospel writers signify what that punishment was. Jesus suffered a severe scourging. This was a whipping with a tool with sharp metal pieces that ripped through the victim's flesh. Some died as consequence of this ordeal. Six hundred years earlier, Isaiah wrote about the suffering servant:

But He was wounded for our transgressions,
He was bruised for our iniquities;
The chastisement for our peace was upon Him,
And by His stripes we are healed. (Isaiah 53:5)

Luke 23:26-43

26 Now as they led Him away, they laid hold of a certain man, Simon a Cyrenian, who was coming from the country, and on him they laid the cross that he might bear *it* after Jesus. **27** And a great multitude of the people followed Him, and women who also mourned and lamented Him. **28** But Jesus, turning to them, said, "Daughters of Jerusalem, do not weep for Me, but weep for yourselves and for your children. **29** For indeed the days are coming in which they will say, 'Blessed *are* the barren, wombs that never bore, and breasts which never nursed!' **30** Then they will begin 'to say to the mountains, "Fall on us!" and to the hills, "Cover us!"' **31** For if they do these things in the green wood, what will be done in the dry?" **32** There were also two others, criminals, led with Him to be put to death. **33** And when they had come to the place called Calvary, there they crucified Him, and the criminals, one on the right hand and the other on the left. **34** Then Jesus said, "Father, forgive them, for they do not know what they do." And they divided His garments and cast lots. **35** And the people stood looking on. But even the rulers with them sneered, saying, "He saved others; let Him save Himself if He is the Christ, the chosen of God." **36** The soldiers also mocked Him, coming and offering Him sour wine, **37** and saying, "If You are the King of the Jews, save Yourself." **38** And an inscription also was written over Him in letters of Greek, Latin, and Hebrew: THIS IS THE KING OF THE JEWS. **39** Then one of the criminals who were hanged blasphemed Him, saying, "If You are the Christ, save Yourself and us." **40** But the other, answering, rebuked him, saying, "Do you not even fear God, seeing you are under the same condemnation? **41** And we indeed justly, for we receive the due reward of our deeds; but this Man has done nothing wrong." **42** Then he said to Jesus, "Lord, remember me when You come into Your kingdom." **43** And Jesus said to him, "Assuredly, I say to you, today you will be with Me in Paradise."

Jesus, like other convicted men, was forced to carry His cross. Victims usually carried the cross beam which could weigh between fifteen and twenty kilograms. Simon of Cyrene was known to the early church in Rome (Mark 15:21) and at some stage, possibly after the resurrection, became a believer. Believers including those from Cyrene and Cyprus planted the important church in Syrian Antioch. (Acts 11:20) Simon was taken out of the crowd and forced to carry the cross. It was something he never forgot. Figuratively speaking, Jesus invited us to identify with Him and carry our cross daily. (Luke 9:23)

Clearly, not all the crowd sought the death of Jesus. A large number of people including women followed Him in great distress.

At this point, it may be said that in the Gospels, no women were critics or accusers of Jesus. The only two who could be described as being in that category were Herodias and Salome who sought the death of John the Baptist. On the whole, women have been more receptive to the Gospel than men.

Jesus turned to them and warned once again, about the destruction of Jerusalem that would come about in AD 70.

As has been stated earlier, all the prophesies of the Bible have and will come true. We do not have a total understanding as to details and how all these things will happen, but we are invited to be aware and ready. (Luke 12:40)

Film-makers and artists have explicitly portrayed the appalling violence of crucifixion.

Some, including Catholics and Moravians have contemplated the sufferings of Christ as a form of devotion. The emotions of such exercises are profound and in some cases led to self-beating and the mysterious origin of stigmata or wounds on the hands and feet. Although the Gospels are plain as to what happened, they do not dramatize the graphic details.

Jesus was not alone in His death. Two criminals accompanied Him. The humiliation could not be more complete and yet Jesus prayed for forgiveness for His executioners. This example has passed down the centuries and repeated by Christian martyrs. Such prayers have brought some of the most violent men into the kingdom. (Acts 7:60)

The onlookers who jeered at Jesus have their words recorded. The words are full of irony. They even acknowledged that He saved others. They added, "Let Him save Himself." They mocked the titles, "Christ, the chosen of God," and "The King of the Jews." Little did they realize as the writer sought to affirm, that Jesus does not save Himself because on the cross He saves others. Moreover, Jesus really is the Christ, the chosen of God, and He really is the King of the Jews.

The other two criminals crucified with Jesus hurled abuse at Him. Then one of them changed his attitude. He might have seen or heard something during Jesus' ministry. Something of the demeanour of Jesus and the conviction of the Holy Spirit worked in the heart of this man.

He rebuked his fellow criminal and asked Jesus to remember him. He came to Christ in the most appalling of circumstances, and yet it is a similar path we all have to take when we become Christians. We have to acknowledge our guilt and the justice of God's judgment. We are to leave behind the mocking attitudes of those around us. We ask Jesus to accept us into His kingdom. As long as the church exists, the model of repentance of the dying thief will always be remembered.

To be in Paradise is to be with Christ. His forgiveness and righteousness are sufficient to allow all to be with Him forever. There is no need for further preparation or purgatory, as some falsely claim.

Luke 23:44-56

44 Now it was about the sixth hour, and there was darkness over all the earth until the ninth hour. **45** Then the sun was darkened, and the veil of the temple was torn in two. **46** And when Jesus had cried out with a loud voice, He said, "Father, 'into Your hands I commit My spirit.'" Having said this, He breathed His last. **47** So when the centurion saw what had happened, he glorified God, saying, "Certainly this was a righteous Man!" **48** And the whole crowd who came together to that sight, seeing what had been done, beat their breasts and returned. **49** But all His acquaintances, and the women who followed Him from Galilee, stood at a distance, watching these things. **50** Now behold, *there was* a man named Joseph, a council member, a good and just man. **51** He had not consented to their decision and deed. *He was* from Arimathea, a city of the Jews, who himself was also waiting for the kingdom of God. **52** This man went to Pilate and asked for the body of Jesus. **53** Then he took it down, wrapped it in linen, and laid it in a tomb *that was* hewn out of the rock, where no one had ever lain before. **54** That day was the Preparation, and the Sabbath drew near. **55** And the women who had come with Him from Galilee followed after, and they observed the tomb and how His body was laid. **56** Then they returned and prepared spices and fragrant oils. And they rested on the Sabbath according to the commandment.

Jesus was on the cross for about three to six hours. There has been much written about the medical aspects of crucifixion, and the cause of death.

There are a number of theories which are summarized here, as simply as possible.

The first is that during crucifixion there is an inability to breathe because of the pain caused to the pierced wrists and hands and feet in the process of respiration. This leads to waterlogging of the lungs or pulmonary oedema. The victims literally drown in their own secretions. That is why the legs were sometimes broken to ensure a rapid death.

Secondly, the presence of excess fluid accumulates around the lining of the heart and causes pressure on the heart so that it is unable to contract properly, and eventually stops.

Thirdly, Jesus may have died from hypovolaemic shock. That is loss of blood and dehydration due to hours of not drinking, and the bleeding associated with severe scourging together with the wounds of crucifixion.

Fourthly, Jesus may have suffered a heart attack or cardiac arrest due to an abnormality that had developed in the muscle or nerve supply to the heart. He may have suffered the first episode on His way to Calvary, when Simon was forced to carry the cross.

It has to be said that these theories although well-informed and suggested by highly trained scientists are somewhat speculative. Some scientists believe that until studies, including modern post-mortem studies, are carried out on crucified subjects, all theories are at best, guesswork. Such studies are of course out of the question.

The Gospel writers do not concern themselves with this kind of detail. Although it is not stated directly, there is an implication in the text that Jesus died at the time of His own choosing. Death had no claim on Him. He laid down His life.

Jesus had completed His sacrifice for the sin of the people, and had been victorious over the devil in that He had secured salvation for humanity. When all this had been done, He could at last commit His Spirit to the Father.

The temple curtain was torn around the time of Jesus' death. The curtain was estimated to be nearly twenty metres high and ten centimetres thick. The rent from top to bottom was drama of profound significance concerning the meaning of the cross. Up to that time, only the high priest was allowed to enter the Holy of Holies once a year on the Day of Atonement. With the opening, a way was now available for believers through Christ to come to God by faith. The book of Hebrews gives us wonderful insights into its significance:

Therefore, brethren, having boldness to enter the Holiest by the blood of

Jesus, by a new and living way which He consecrated for us, through the veil, that is, His flesh, and having a High Priest over the house of God, let us draw near with a true heart in full assurance of faith, having our hearts sprinkled from an evil conscience and our bodies washed with pure water. Let us hold fast the confession of our hope without wavering, for He who promised is faithful. (Hebrews 10:19-23)

Luke in relating this event made an invitation to readers to believe in Christ.

It is ironic that the first person to make a pronouncement was a Gentile – the Roman centurion in charge of the crucifixion squad. He declared Jesus to be a "righteous man", or the "righteous one". (v. 47) He may not have understood the full meaning of his statement, but the Gospel writers certainly chose to emphasize it.

Years ago in the UK, there were public hangings. The last one was in 1868. People turned up for the spectacle and to cheer the death of a murderer.

When Jesus died on the cross, people gathered to see the spectacle but the mood became very sombre as many realized, as they departed, the iniquity of what had happened. This is a prequel to the attitudes of many in latter days:

They shall look on Him whom they pierced. (John 19:37)

Behold, He is coming with clouds, and every eye will see Him, even they who pierced Him. And all the tribes of the earth will mourn because of Him. (Revelation 1: 7)

Those who knew Jesus were frightened and stood away at a distance.

Joseph of Arimathea, a member of the assembly is a signal to us that not every member of an apparently hostile group follows that group. He was wealthy, educated and humbly seeking the kingdom of God. He was willing to take a risk and ask Pilate for the body of Jesus. The crucified were usually dumped on a heap to be disposed of by dogs and other scavengers.

Joseph set aside a tomb meant for himself, to give some final dignity to the one he had come to believe in.

The little details of the passage sound like an eyewitness account given in person to Luke. Luke wanted to emphasize that Jesus had died and that His body had been wrapped up and placed in a tomb. The place had been noted to emphasize that there had been no mistake as to its location.

Once again we see a crucial contribution of devout women in the story. They were faithful, loyal and courageous. If others had denied respect to their Lord, they were going to honour the body with expensive embalming spices, no matter the cost to them financially and to their reputation. No first century writer would have given women such an important place in the story if it had been a fabrication.

Luke 24:1-35

1 Now on the first *day* of the week, very early in the morning, they, and certain *other women* with them, came to the tomb bringing the spices which they had prepared. 2 But they found the stone rolled away from the tomb. 3 Then they went in and did not find the body of the Lord Jesus. 4 And it happened, as they were greatly perplexed about this, that behold, two men stood by them in shining garments. 5 Then, as they were afraid and bowed *their* faces to the earth, they said to them, "Why do you seek the living among the dead? 6 He is not here, but is risen! Remember how He spoke to you when He was still in Galilee, 7 saying, 'The Son of Man must be delivered into the hands of sinful men, and be crucified, and the third day rise again.'" 8 And they remembered His words. 9 Then they returned from the tomb and told all these things to the eleven and to all the rest. 10 It was Mary Magdalene, Joanna, Mary *the mother* of James, and the other *women* with them, who told these things to the apostles. 11 And their words seemed to them like idle tales, and they did not believe them. 12 But Peter arose and ran to the tomb; and stooping down, he saw the linen cloths lying by themselves; and he departed, marveling to himself at what had happened. 13 Now behold, two of them were traveling that same day to a village called Emmaus, which was seven miles from Jerusalem. 14 And they talked together of all these things which had happened. 15 So it was, while they conversed and reasoned, that Jesus Himself drew near and went with them. 16 But their eyes were restrained, so that they did not know Him. 17 And He said to them, "What kind of conversation *is* this that you have with one another as you walk and are sad?" 18 Then the one whose name was Cleopas answered and said to Him, "Are You the only stranger in Jerusalem, and have You not known the things which happened there in these days?" 19 And He said to them, "What things?" So they said to Him, "The things concerning Jesus of Nazareth, who was a Prophet mighty in deed and word before God and all the people, 20 and how the chief priests and our rulers delivered Him to be condemned to death, and crucified Him. 21 But we were hoping that it was He who was going to redeem Israel. Indeed, besides all this, today is the third day since these things happened. 22 Yes, and certain women of our company, who arrived at the tomb early, astonished us. 23 When they did not find His body, they came saying that they had also seen a vision of angels who said He was alive. 24 And certain of those *who were* with us went to the

tomb and found *it* just as the women had said; but Him they did not see." **25** Then He said to them, "O foolish ones, and slow of heart to believe in all that the prophets have spoken! **26** Ought not the Christ to have suffered these things and to enter into His glory?" **27** And beginning at Moses and all the Prophets, He expounded to them in all the Scriptures the things concerning Himself. **28** Then they drew near to the village where they were going, and He indicated that He would have gone farther. **29** But they constrained Him, saying, "Abide with us, for it is toward evening, and the day is far spent." And He went in to stay with them. **30** Now it came to pass, as He sat at the table with them, that He took bread, blessed and broke *it,* and gave it to them. **31** Then their eyes were opened and they knew Him; and He vanished from their sight. **32** And they said to one another, "Did not our heart burn within us while He talked with us on the road, and while He opened the Scriptures to us?" **33** So they rose up that very hour and returned to Jerusalem, and found the eleven and those *who were* with them gathered together, **34** saying, "The Lord is risen indeed, and has appeared to Simon!" **35** And they told about the things *that had happened* on the road, and how He was known to them in the breaking of bread.

In this Chapter, Luke sought to establish a number of facts about the resurrection. First of all, He stated the day and the approximate time. He went on to say that with a particular task in mind, some women visited the tomb, three of whom were named. He established that the stone had been moved and that the tomb was empty.

He then described the appearance of angels which prompted a sense of fear. Angels were present at the birth of Christ, (Luke 2:13) and they were present at His resurrection. (v. 4)

The message was of key importance. Jesus was not there because He had risen. It was as Jesus had described during His ministry. Luke insisted that the news was totally unexpected and that even after this reminder the male disciples in their chauvinistic manner thought that the women's account was complete nonsense.

Nevertheless, Peter, in typical action man mode, ran to the tomb and saw the pattern of the remaining grave cloths and left feeling puzzled. Other Gospel writers give more detail to the story, but Luke wanted to make clear at that point all the relevant facts that the reader needs to know.

In doing so he countered various theories that skeptics have produced to deny the resurrection. The early one that the disciples stole the body, (Matthew 28: 12-15) is refuted by the fact that the disciples had scattered in fear and were in obvious disbelief and disarray.

A later "swoon" theory that Jesus had not died may sound plausible because most victims usually took longer to die on a cross than He did. This does not stand up scrutiny because Jesus would have had to have survived scourging which, as has been said, could alone have been fatal. This was followed by crucifixion. All this was added to sixty hours without food, drink or medical attention. On recovery He would have had to release Himself from the cloth and roll away a massively heavy stone. What seems initially plausible becomes totally implausible on examination.

The Muslim theory that Jesus was exchanged for another, possibly Simon of Cyrene, appears to be a fanciful construction in view of the narrative and evidence of Luke and the others.

Luke then moved the story to the afternoon, and introduces us to two new characters. They also were in a dark state of grief, disillusionment, and disappointment. All their time, hopes and expectations about Jesus had come to nothing.

A fellow traveller joined them on the road and appeared not to be aware of the latest tragic news. Jesus had publicly taught in the temple, and had been crucified for all Jerusalem to see. The two explained their sorrow at their failed hope that Jesus was going to redeem Israel politically. Then they described incredulously the strange events that morning around the tomb. The traveller then began to explain from the Scriptures what kind of Messiah was foretold. The Scriptures were about a suffering Messiah and then a glorified Messiah.

Jesus quoted the Old Testament Scriptures and emphasized their inspiration and importance. If Jesus did that, so should we. I like the comment that we should read and examine the Old Testament through a New Testament lens. That is, we should interpret it in light of the teachings of Jesus.

Many have wished to know what Jesus said on that three or so hours walk. However, it can be reckoned that much of the subject matter would have been part of the sermons contained in Acts, together with much of the material in the Epistles.

Jesus gave the impression that He did not wish to stay but He was urged to stay. (v.29) Jesus still loves our entreaties for Him to stay with us and never leave us.

The fact that Jesus was not recognized until the breaking of bread is full of mystery. There are suggested possible physical reasons for this but there is some significance in that we do not recognize Him truly until we have heard the message of the Gospel and have asked Him into our lives.

Their hasty return to find the eleven in Jerusalem is evidence of both their conviction and excitement.

Luke 24:36-53

36 Now as they said these things, Jesus Himself stood in the midst of them, and said to them, "Peace to you." **37** But they were terrified and frightened, and supposed they had seen a spirit. **38** And He said to them, "Why are you troubled? And why do doubts arise in your hearts? **39** Behold My hands and My feet, that it is I Myself. Handle Me and see, for a spirit does not have flesh and bones as you see I have." **40** When He had said this, He showed them His hands and His feet. **41** But while they still did not believe for joy, and marveled, He said to them, "Have you any food here?" **42** So they gave Him a piece of a broiled fish and some honeycomb. **43** And He took *it* and ate in their presence. **44** Then He said to them, "These *are* the words which I spoke to you while I was still with you, that all things must be fulfilled which were written in the Law of Moses and *the* Prophets and *the* Psalms concerning Me." **45** And He opened their understanding, that they might comprehend the Scriptures. **46** Then He said to them, "Thus it is written, and thus it was necessary for the Christ to suffer and to rise from the dead the third day, **47** and that repentance and remission of sins should be preached in His name to all nations, beginning at Jerusalem. **48** And you are witnesses of these things. **49** Behold, I send the Promise of My Father upon you; but tarry in the city of Jerusalem until you are endued with power from on high." **50** And He led them out as far as Bethany, and He lifted up His hands and blessed them. **51** Now it came to pass, while He blessed them, that He was parted from them and carried up into heaven. **52** And they worshiped Him, and returned to Jerusalem with great joy, **53** and were continually in the temple praising and blessing God. Amen

In all, the Gospels record eleven resurrection appearances of our Lord. Luke describes four of them of which this is his third. Again he answers the critic or the attempted rational explanation. The disciples themselves, far from being gullible, could hardly believe their senses. There is a possible explanation that they saw a ghost or had a group hallucination. In other words, this may have been like visions of the Virgin Mary. Such visions have happened in recent times in various parts of the world but have only been experienced by the visionaries and not others present on the scene. This is discounted by Jesus' touch, the showing of His marked hands and feet, and the eating of fish.

Another possibility that has been suggested is that the disciples had dreams and years later made it into a resurrection story. When we lose a close loved relative or friend, we often have vivid dreams of them coming to us and talking to us, especially at times when important decisions have to be made. I experienced this a few times following the death of my first wife. Special as they were, I woke up afterwards and knew they were dreams. If the disciples experienced dreams, they were the type of people to acknowledge them as just that, dreams. It is impossible to launch the enterprise that the disciples did on the basis of dreams and hallucinations.

In this passage we see something of the nature of Jesus and the disciples. Firstly, we note the kindness of Christ. He did not admonish them for their unbelief or backsliding. He was gentle with them and said, "Peace to you." He invited them into His confidence and friendship. Since then, Jesus has extended that invitation to all who seek to believe in Him.

The disciples moved from fear, to amazement and then to joy. Christians throughout the history of the church have experienced these emotions.

There is often a wonder and fear when contemplating the awesome vastness and complexity of the Universe and our minute and fragile role within it. When we realize the holiness and judgment of God, that also is a time to fear.

Then we can be amazed that the Creator of that Universe should bring humanity into being, and be interested in our lives and destiny. Then we become full of joy that He should love us and allow things that lead to our ultimate and eternal good, even though some of the way may be hard and painful.

The appearance of Jesus also demonstrates the importance of teaching. Jesus' prime purpose in His ministry was to teach. (Luke 4: 43) Here, He taught them once again the significance of His death and resurrection and their relationship to the Old Testament. This time, the message began to really sink in. At last they understood. Let us pray to the Father that we will understand all the things about Him that need to be taught and known.

Then the disciples were given an overwhelming task. They were to begin in Jerusalem and then go into the whole world and spread the message they had heard. Jesus emphasized the need for repentance and forgiveness. There are many important things in life such as education, sound relationships, purposeful work and a sense of worth, but the most important things are repentance and forgiveness.

The church has taken centuries to preach the Gospel to all nations, and we still have not finished. What a task, but again Jesus reminded them of the Holy Spirit who would be present with all His people.

On the final appearance He blessed them as He continues to bless us. They worshiped Him as they would worship God because they knew that He was God. Then He was taken up. The angels greeted the birth of Jesus with "tidings of great joy". (Luke 2:10) That joy was now in the hearts of believers. (v.v. 52-53)

Luke closed his Gospel at that point. He did not put his pen down but continued the narrative of Christ in "The Acts of the Apostles". In fact, these were acts of Jesus through the Holy Spirit and the work of His people.